UNDERSTANDING INFLATION & UNEMPLOYMENT

ALLEN W. SMITH

Nelson-Hall nh Chicago

Library of Congress Cataloging in Publication Data

Smith, Allen William.
   Understanding inflation & unemployment.

   Includes index.
     1. Inflation (Finance)—United States.   2. Un-
employed—United States.   3. Fiscal policy—United
States.   4. Monetary policy—United States.   I. Title.
HG538.S585   332.4'1'0973   75-29492
ISBN 0-88229-276-5

To
Deanna, Mark, Michael and Lisa

Contents

Preface

Inflation and unemployment are both extremely serious economic problems. Furthermore, they are tied together in the sense that there is a tradeoff relationship between the two. Since efforts to reduce one usually contribute to an increase in the other, economic policy makers are faced with a serious dilemma. Which of these two economic ills should receive the higher priority? Since the economic health of the nation is dependent upon keeping both under control, there is no easy answer to this priority question.

In a democracy, major problems cannot be solved without the support of the electorate. However, there are few political issues today which generate more confusion and misinformation than economic policies. Most Americans have never had an introductory course in basic economics. Furthermore, there are few books available on the subject which do not require previous formal study in economics. Too often, economists seem to write for other economists, using technical language and analysis which are unintelligible to the layman.

This book is written for both laymen and students. It is nontechnical; the layman with no previous training in economics should be able to master its contents. I have avoided the use of graphical models in the basic text of the book in favor of a simplified verbal presentation. However, certain basic models commonly used in economic analysis have been included in the appendix for those who desire a more technical comprehension of the subject.

Although the book is not intended as a basic textbook for an economics course, I believe it can be useful as a nontechnical supplement to the more traditional basic economics textbook. Too often students get so sidetracked in mastering the details and technical analyses of a comprehensive textbook that they fail to understand the basic economic concepts underlying the details. This book provides a fairly comprehensive survey of the basic economic concepts underlying the problems of inflation and unemployment while avoiding the technical details.

I have deliberately restricted the scope of the book in order to keep it as concise and readable as possible. There are many comprehensive books available for the reader who desires detail and technical analysis in order to gain a more comprehensive knowledge of the subject. My purpose is to present the fundamentals of the inflation and unemployment problems as concisely as possible. Through this abbreviated approach, I believe the reader can gain considerable comprehension of an important subject with a minimum investment of time.

1 The Inflation & Unemployment Problems

Although there is general agreement that inflation and unemployment are both bad and should be avoided if possible, there is considerable disagreement over which of the two is more harmful. Since a certain amount of inflation and/or unemployment is unavoidable, and since efforts to reduce one usually result in an increase in the other, the question of which is more harmful becomes relevant.

The Effects of Inflation

Inflation may be defined in a variety of ways. For my purpose inflation is defined as a general rise in the price level or, to put it another way, a decline in the purchasing-power of the dollar. A more comprehensive analysis of types and causes of inflation will be made in the next chapter. My purpose here is to examine the negative effects of inflation.

Effects on Income Distribution

Inflation tends to benefit some individuals at the expense of others. While for some income receivers income rises more rapidly than prices during inflation, for many individuals just the opposite is true. Many older retired people live on fixed incomes. Their money incomes remain constant while prices are rising. Thus, they experience a decline in real income[1] during inflation. If serious inflation persists for a prolonged period, these people find themselves in serious financial trouble. For example, if over a period of years the price level doubles, those individuals on fixed incomes will find that their real income has been cut in half.

Another group, less severely affected, includes teachers, civil service employees, and others who find that their incomes usually rise less rapidly than prices during periods of inflation. While this group is less seriously affected than those who are on fixed incomes, real income does usually decline during periods of inflation.

Effects on Long-Term Lending

Inflation benefits borrowers at the expense of the lenders. Suppose you borrow $10,000 which you promise to repay at the end of two years. If prices were to double during the two-year period, you would in effect be paying back only $5,000 in purchasing power. Although you repay $10,000 in money terms, this $10,000 will buy only as much as $5,000 would have bought before prices doubled.

Although this is an extreme example, the problem is very real. Today there are many long-term mortgage loans outstanding with an interest rate as low as 6 percent. If the inflation rate is 6 percent, the lender will in effect

---

[1]Real income is a measure of the purchasing power of money income.

receive no interest income on the loan. With an inflation rate of 6 percent, it would take a 6 percent interest rate just for the lender to maintain the purchasing power of the money he has loaned. There would be nothing left for interest income. When the inflation rate rises above 6 percent as it did in 1973 and 1974, the lender is actually losing money on a 6 percent loan.

Lenders have in the past been willing to make long-term loans at a fixed interest rate because they had faith in the government's ability to maintain relatively stable prices over the long run. Most periods of inflation in the past have not lasted very long. However, if lenders lose confidence in the government's ability to control inflation, they may be unwilling in the future to make long-term loans at a fixed interest rate. It may become necessary for the potential home buyer to agree to a fluctuating interest rate tied to the inflation index, or to receive only short-term financing which would have to be renewed periodically at the then current market rate of interest.

Effects on Savings

The effect on savers is identical to the effect on lenders. In a sense, when an individual deposits money in his savings account he is lending the money to the bank. Suppose you deposit $100 in a savings account for one year at 5 percent interest. At the end of the year you can withdraw the $100 plus $5 in interest earnings. Will the $105 at the end of the year buy more than the $100 would have when you deposited it at the beginning of the year? If the price level rose by less than 5 percent during the year, you have made some gain. However, if the price level rose by 5 percent during the year, you have just broken even. The $105 at the end of the year will buy the same amount that $100 would have bought at the beginning of the year. In effect, you receive no interest income. If the price level rises by more than 5 percent, the value of your savings decreases. Thus, the interest rate must be at least as high as the inflation rate just to maintain the purchasing power of your savings. The interest rate must be higher than the inflation rate in order to receive any interest income in real terms.

A retired individual who must live off the interest earnings of his or her savings is very seriously affected by prolonged inflation. If over a period of years the price level doubles, the value of savings is cut in half. This can be disastrous for those who have no other source of income except from their savings.

Effects on World Trade

An often ignored effect of inflation is the impact that rising prices have on world trade. To the extent that prices in the United States rise more rapidly than prices in other countries, our competitiveness in world markets is reduced. The international balance of payments problem facing the United States today is extremely complex and is due to a number of factors. However, the extensive inflation of recent years has certainly contributed to the problem.

The Effects of Unemployment

Unemployment is one of the most serious problems facing the American economy in terms of both economic and social costs. Let us examine some of the disastrous effects of unemployment.

Direct Economic Costs to the Nation

The direct economic cost to the nation is the loss in output that occurs during unemployment. Even moderate unemployment can cost the nation billions of dollars in lost production, and the costs of a serious recession or depression are almost beyond comprehension. The lost production that resulted from the great depression of the 1930s amounted to hundreds of billions of dollars, and can never be made up. Men, factories, and other resources sat idle during this period when they could have been producing billions of dollars worth of goods and services if the economy had been functioning properly. The long-term cost to the economy was astronomical.

Social Consequences

Unemployment is a social catastrophe as well as an economic one. The social costs cannot always be measured in dollar terms, but they involve an intolerable amount of human suffering. Unemployment means idleness, loss of self-respect, poverty, and fear to those individuals who are jobless. In addition to those who are without any work, millions of others are reduced to part-time jobs during a period of unemployment. Furthermore, millions of workers who do not lose their jobs live in constant fear that they will soon join the ranks of the unemployed.

The costs of unemployment are not shared equally by all the nation's citizens. Certain groups and certain geographic areas are more likely to experience unemployment that others. When the government reports a national unemployment rate of 8 percent this is simply a national average. Many groups and many geographic areas will have unemployment rates substantially above the national average. For example, the unemployment rate for the nation as a whole for January 1975 was 8.2 percent. Yet, teenagers experienced an unemployment rate of 20.8 percent while men, twenty years old and older, had an unemployment rate of only 6.0 percent. A more detailed breakdown of unemployment rates by color, sex, and age can be seen in Table 1. You will note that unemployment rates are higher for nonwhites, women, and teenagers than for whites, men, and nonteenagers.

Table 1
Seasonally Adjusted Unemployment
Rates by Color, Sex, and Age
January 1975

Characteristic	Unemployment Rate (percent)
White	
Civilian Labor Force	7.5
Negro and Other Races	
Civilian Labor Force	13.4
Total	
Civilian Labor Force	8.2
Men, 20 Years and Over	6.0
Women, 20 Years and Over	8.1
Both Sexes, 16-19 Years	20.8

Source: U.S. Department of Labor, *Monthly Labor Review.*

Certain geographic areas of the country experience unemployment rates considerably above the national average at any given point in time, while other areas have rates below the national average. In Table 2 unemployment rates for selected geographic areas are presented to emphasize the wide range in unemployment rates. You will note that the unemployment rate for the nation as a whole in February 1974 was 5.2 percent. However, local unemployment rates ranged as high as 17.0 percent in Flint, Michigan, and as low as 1.8 percent in Charlotte, North Carolina, during the same month.

, Some local areas experience unemployment rates consistently above or below the national average. However, other areas experience considerable fluctuations in their unemployment rates and are sometimes above and sometimes below the national average. For example, Flint, Michigan, had an unemployment rate of 4.7 percent in February 1973 and an unemployment rate of 17.0 percent one year later. This rapid increase in unemployment was probably due to the severe impact on

Table 2
Unemployment Rates for Selected
Labor Areas
February, 1974

Area	Unemployment Rate (percent)
United States	5.2
Stockton, California	10.0
Denver, Colorado	2.8
Hartford, Connecticut	5.1
Jacksonville, Florida	2.5
Chicago, Illinois	3.6
Cedar Rapids, Iowa	2.4
Baltimore, Maryland	2.9
Fall River, Massachusetts	9.0
Flint, Michigan	17.0
Saginaw, Michigan	10.0
Jackson, Mississippi	2.7
St. Louis, Missouri	5.4
Buffalo, New York	9.3
Charlotte, North Carolina	1.8
Portland, Oregon	5.2
Austin, Texas	2.3
Tacoma, Washington	9.1

Source: U.S. Department of Labor, *Area Trends in Employment and Unemployment.*

the automobile industry resulting from the energy crisis of 1973-74. Almost everybody was in some way affected by the energy crisis. However, we did not share equally in its costs. Those individuals who lost their jobs paid a much higher price than most of us. Such is always the case with unemployment, regardless of its cause. The nation as a whole pays a price, but some individuals pay a higher price than others.

The Inflation-Unemployment Tradeoff Problem

In the preceding sections we have emphasized the heavy costs of both inflation and unemployment. Obviously, it would be extremely desirable to eliminate both unemployment and inflation. Unfortunately, such a course of action is not possible. In an economy such as ours, a certain amount of inflation and/or unemployment is unavoidable.

It might be possible to reduce the inflation rate to near zero. However, the cost of such an action would be much higher unemployment. On the other hand, it might be possible to bring the economy close to the full-employment level, but this would result in substantial inflation. Thus, policy makers face a serious dilemma. Efforts to reduce unemployment usually result in increased inflation, while efforts to reduce inflation usually bring about an increase in the jobless rate.

The inflation-unemployment tradeoff problem is frequently presented graphically in the form of a "Phillips curve," named after its originator, Australian economist A.W. Phillips. The Phillips curve in Figure 1 illustrates the inflation-unemployment tradeoff. The relationship between inflation and unemployment is not stable or precise. Therefore, any graphic presentation must be only an approximation. Figure 1 should be considered as an example of a tradeoff relationship rather than a portrayal of the actual relationship in the United States. The tradeoff relationship in Figure 1 suggests that in order to have zero inflation it would be necessary to have a 6 percent unemployment rate. It also suggests that efforts to lower the unemployment rate below 6 percent will result in inflation. As the economy is pushed closer and closer to full employment (3 to 4 percent unemployment is generally considered full employment), the inflation rate increases more and more.

Thus, the Phillips curve suggests that several options are open to the policy makers. They can choose (1) stable prices with high unemployment, (2) full employment with high inflation, or (3) some combination of inflation and unemployment between the two extremes. The policy

Figure 1
The Inflation-Unemployment Tradeoff
Problem

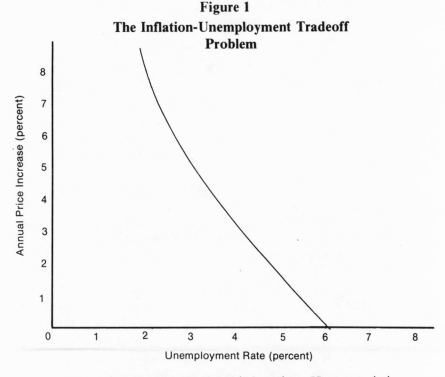

makers usually choose the third option. However, it is difficult to get agreement on the exact combination of inflation and unemployment which should be set as the target of economic policy.

The reasons for the tradeoff relationship will be presented in more detail later. In brief, they involve the level of total spending in the economy. A remedy for unemployment is increased spending. However, when spending increases, prices tend to rise. On the other hand, one method of reducing inflation is to reduce the level of total spending. But when total spending is reduced, sales decline, inventories build up, and workers are dismissed. Just as one man's medicine is another man's poison, actions taken to solve the unemployment problem usually increase the inflation problem, and actions taken to reduce inflation usually increase unemployment.

The Inflation-Unemployment Record for the United States

Over the years the United States has experienced periods of high inflation and periods of high unemployment, but the nation has seldom faced a problem of both high inflation and high unemployment at the same time. The simultaneous combination of high inflation and high unemployment which began in 1970 and continues today is unique in recent American history. Consumer price data and unemployment data for the United States from 1953 through 1974 are presented in Table 3. A careful examination of the data will reveal that there are no periods of both substantial inflation and unemployment prior to 1970.

The data have been grouped into four periods: 1953-57, 1958-65, 1966-69, and 1970-74. Since full employment is generally considered to be in the neighborhood of 3 to 4 percent unemployment, the five-year period 1953 through 1957 can be described as having generally low rates of both unemployment and inflation. However, there are two exceptions to the pattern. In 1954 the unemployment rate climbed to 5.5 percent, but this was accompanied by an inflation rate of only .5 percent. Also, in 1957 the inflation rate was 3.6 percent, but unemployment was only 4.3 percent.

The eight-year period 1958 through 1965 follows a very consistent pattern. High rates of unemployment are combined with relatively low rates of inflation. In all but the last year of the eight-year period the annual unemployment rate was above 5 percent, with two years above 6.5 percent unemployment. On the inflation side, seven of the eight years had an annual inflation rate of less than 2 percent.

During the four-year period 1966 through 1969, the

Table 3
Changes In Consumer Prices and Unemployment Rates for the United States, 1953-1974

Year	Percent Increase[1] in Annual Average Consumer Prices		Percent Unemployment
1953	.8	(Generally low	2.9
1954	.5	rates of both	5.5
1955	-.4	unemployment	4.4
1956	1.5	and inflation)	4.1
1957	3.6		4.3
1958	2.7	(Generally high	6.8
1959	.8	rates of unem-	5.5
1960	1.6	ployment with	5.5
1961	1.0	low rates of	6.7
1962	1.1	inflation)	5.5
1963	1.2		5.7
1964	1.3		5.2
1965	1.7		4.5
1966	2.9	(Very low unem-	3.8
1967	2.9	ployment rates	3.8
1968	4.2	with rising levels	3.6
1969	5.4	of inflation)	3.5
1970	5.9	(High rates of	4.9
1971	4.3	both unemploy-	5.9
1972	3.3	ment and	5.6
1973	6.2	inflation)	4.9
1974	11.0[2]		5.6

[1]Consumer price increases reflect the change in the annual average consumer price index from one year to the next.

[2]During the twelve-month period December 1973 to December 1974 the consumer price index rose by 12.2 percent.

Source: U.S. Department of Labor, *Monthly Labor Review.*

economy was operating near the full employment level for each of the four years. However, the low unemployment rates were accompanied by increasingly higher rates of inflation.

In 1970, the economy began to experience the unusual problem of both high unemployment and high inflation at the same time. This phenomenon will be examined in detail in Chapter 8. For the moment, suffice it to say that the policy makers of the 1970s are faced with more than the tradeoff dilemma. In the past, policy makers were usually confronted with either an unemployment or an inflation problem, but not both at the same time. Today, they must deal with both problems simultaneously.

The Priority Problem

Since actions taken to reduce inflation usually contribute to more unemployment, and actions taken to reduce unemployment usually increase the inflation rate, it is necessary for policy makers to set priorities. Setting priorities with regard to inflation and unemployment is not an easy task. The policy makers are faced with the following questions. Should we always aim for price stability even if it means considerable unemployment? Should our goal be full employment regardless of the cost in terms of inflation? Should we compromise and accept both some inflation and some unemployment rather than a lot of one and none of the other? If we choose a combination of both unemployment and inflation, exactly what should that combination be?

These are difficult questions for which there are no right or wrong answers. The policy makers must use value judgments in determining the policy goals. It is unlikely that any administration would ever choose to put all its emphasis on solving one of these two economic evils while completely ignoring the other. Usually, an effort will be made to avoid extremely high levels of either inflation or unemployment. In other words, policy makers will usually choose to accept both some inflation and some unemployment. However, administrations differ on the relative importance which they place on solving the two problems. For example, the Eisenhower administration put considerable emphasis on maintaining price stability and was willing to pay a rather high price in unemployment to achieve this goal. On the other hand, the Kennedy and Johnson administrations tended to put a higher priority on maintaining full employment than on maintaining price stability, although they were concerned about both.

The relative importance which an administration puts on solving the inflation and unemployment problems depends upon the relative influence of the various interest groups within the economy. For example, labor unions tend to put more emphasis on preventing unemployment than on preventing inflation, because they are usually able to make sufficient wage gains to offset or keep ahead of rising prices. On the other hand, bankers, who are seldom unemployed, are very concerned about maintaining stable prices and the value of the dollar. While they are not unconcerned about unemployment, if they have to make a choice they will usually choose more unemployment and less inflation.

Hence, while there is general agreement that both inflation and unemployment are bad, there is considerable disagreement over which is worse. Therefore, the question of whether greater emphasis should be placed on solving inflation, or unemployment, remains a difficult one which must be answered through the political process.

Summary

1. Although there is general agreement that both inflation and unemployment are harmful, there is considerable disagreement over which is more harmful.

2. A certain amount of inflation and/or unemployment is unavoidable in our economy, and efforts to reduce one usually result in an increase in the other.

3. Inflation can be very costly. It tends to benefit some individuals at the expense of others and causes a

certain amount of income redistribution. It benefits borrowers at the expense of lenders and may threaten long-term lending. Savers are adversely affected by inflation since it decreases the value of savings. Inflation may also decrease our competitiveness in world markets and adversely affect the international balance of payments.

4. Unemployment can be extremely costly in both economic and social terms. The direct economic cost to the nation is the loss in output that occurs during unemployment. The great depression of the 1930s cost the economy hundreds of billions of dollars in lost production. Although the social costs of unemployment cannot always be measured in dollar terms, they involve an intolerable amount of human suffering. The costs of unemployment are not shared equally by all the nation's citizens.

5. Since there is a tradeoff relationship between inflation and unemployment, policy makers are faced with the problem of deciding which of the two problems should receive higher priority.

6. In 1970 the economy began to experience the unusual problem of both high unemployment and high inflation at the same time. This phenomenon, which is unique in recent American history, poses one of the most serious dilemmas in economic history.

2 Types of Inflation & Causes

Although inflation always means rising prices, the rates of inflation and the reasons for the price increases are not always the same. Therefore, several descriptive terms have been coined to refer to different types of inflation.

Different Rates of Inflation

Terms such as "hyperinflation," "runaway inflation," and "galloping inflation" refer to extremely high rates of inflation such as occurred in Germany after World War I. Prices increased a trillionfold in the German inflation of 1920-23, and the post-World War II inflation in Hungary was even worse.

The term "creeping inflation" is frequently used to refer to a slow but persistent rise in the general price level over a period of years, usually at annual rates of 3 percent or less. Terms such as "walking" or "trotting" inflation are sometimes used to describe inflation rates between "creeping inflation" and "hyperinflation."

Different Causes of Inflation

The above terms all refer to rates of inflation. Various other terms are frequently used to describe inflation in terms of the underlying causes. Terms such as "demand-pull," "cost-push," "wage-push," "profit-push," "administered-price," and "structural" inflation are commonly used by economists to describe the type of inflation that is taking place at any given time. Actually, the causes of inflation are usually rather complex. Therefore, none of these terms provides a totally adequate explanation in most cases.

Demand-Pull Inflation

"Demand-pull" inflation occurs when the total spending in the economy rises more rapidly than the available supply of goods and services. In other words, the total spending by consumers, businessmen, and the government exceeds the total supply of goods and services available. Therefore, in the absence of artificial controls prices must necessarily rise.

Structural Inflation

"Structural" inflation is a related concept. However, "structural" inflation can occur even when total demand and total supply for the economy are in balance. As an economy approaches full employment, shortages occur in some industries before others. Thus, excess demand and increasing cost pressures may exist in certain industries even when the total demand for the economy does not exceed the total supply.

The food industry provides an excellent example of the potential for "structural" inflation. Even in times of high unemployment and abnormally low total demand in the economy, food shortages can occur. If poor weather conditions or other factors cause the supply of food to fall short of the demand, prices will tend to rise. This is in a sense "demand-pull" inflation in the food industry. However, since the total dollar demand in the economy does not exceed the total dollar supply of goods and services, the economy as a whole is not experiencing "demand-pull" inflation.

Administered Price Increases

The terms "cost-push," "wage-push," and "profit-push" inflation all refer to "administered" price increases. In other words, prices rise even though there may be no excess demand for the goods and services in question. Producers with strong market power simply raise their prices. If the price increases are motivated by increased production costs, they constitute "cost-push" inflation. If the increased production costs have resulted from increased wages forced upon the producer by a strong labor union, the price increase may be referred to as "wage-push" inflation. However, if the price increase is motivated by the producer's desire to increase his profits, it is "profit-push" inflation. "Cost-push," "wage-push," and "profit-push" inflation all involve the same thing— "administered" price increases. The various terms simply describe the motivation for the price increases. Therefore, throughout the remainder of this book we shall refer to all three collectively as "administered-price" inflation.

Excess Demand and Market Adjustments

Excess demand occurs when the demand for a good or service exceeds the available supply. Suppose an item is offered for sale at an auction. If only one individual attending the auction has a strong desire to possess that item, the price will probably be quite low. But suppose two individuals at the auction are determined to buy the one item. In this case, the price will be bid up to a level where the individual with the lesser determination to possess the item decides to stop bidding. If three bidders are intent on having the single item, the price will rise even higher. In other words, any time the demand for any good or service is greater than the quantity available, the price will tend to rise if there are no artificial restrictions on the price.

Although rising prices are usually unpopular with most people, they do serve a useful purpose in a free market economy. Prices serve as a rationing device. What determines which of the three bidders at the auction will get the one scarce item? The answer, of course, is that the individual who is willing to pay the highest price will get the item. The price will continue to rise until two of the bidders decide that they no longer want the item if they must pay such a high price. Thus, the price system has equated supply and demand by adjusting to such a level that only one individual wants the one scarce item at the final auction price.

Of course individual wealth and income play an important role in the rationing process. It may be that the highest bidder in our auction example is not the most deserving of the three, or even the one with the strongest desire for the object. He may simply be the only one who can afford to pay the high price which the object brings under the competitive bidding. Hence, while the rationing process of the market system may be an effective way of determining who gets what, it may not always be equitable. For this reason, many government programs are aimed at bringing about a more equitable distribution of income.

There will probably always be excess demand for some items in our economy. However, the items in short supply will not always be the same ones. In addition to rationing out the scarce items, rising prices often encourage additional production, thus alleviating the shortage and sometimes resulting in lower prices.

An excellent example of this process is found in the production of meat. When there is a shortage of pork, and prices rise, farmers find it more profitable to produce pork and thus increase production. As the additional supply of pork reaches the market, prices will tend to level off or possibly even decline.

Thus, in some cases a shortage leads to higher prices, which lead to additional production, which leads to an alleviation of the shortage and possibly even lower prices. In the case of pork and beef production the cycle may repeat itself over and over. The alleviation of the shortage may result in such low prices for the farmer that he will tend to reduce production. This may lead to another shortage, which will start the whole adjustment process over again.

In a dynamic free market economy there will always tend to be shortages of some things at any given point in time. However, there will also always tend to be surpluses of some things. To the extent that the surpluses offset the shortages, there is no excess demand for the economy as a whole. In other words, the economy is producing more than enough of some items even though shortages do exist for certain other items. If prices are falling in those areas where there are surpluses, these price declines may offset the price increases where shortages exist and thus prevent a general inflation for the economy as a whole. Thus, the absence of inflation does not necessarily mean that no prices are rising. It simply means that prices on the average are stable. Increased prices for pork may be offset by reduced prices for potatoes and eggs.

The most frequently used measure of inflation is the consumer price index. This index measures the increase in the cost of a "package" of some four hundred items selected by the United States Bureau of Labor Statistics as a "typical basket" of goods and services purchased by consumers. If the average consumer price index rises, then inflation is occurring even though the prices of some items included in the index are falling. The declining prices are more than offset by rising prices for other items. On the other hand, if the average consumer price index remains stable, no general inflation is occurring even though some prices are rising.

Excess Demand for the Economy and Demand-Pull Inflation

In the preceding section examples were given of rising prices for specific items which were caused by excess demand for those specific items. In a dynamic economy market adjustments will always be taking place, with increasing demand in some markets and decreasing demand in others. To the extent that decreasing demand in some markets offsets the increasing demand in other markets, the general price level in the economy may be relatively stable. In other words, prices for some items may be falling at the same time that other prices are rising.

A general "demand-pull" inflation occurs when the increasing demand in expanding industries more than offsets any decreasing demand that may be taking place in contracting industries. In other words, the total demand for goods and services exceeds the productive capacity of the economy.

The total output of goods and services produced by the U.S. economy is measured by the Gross National Product (GNP). The GNP is defined as the total dollar value of all goods and services produced by the economy in a year's time, measured in terms of their market prices. Hence, the GNP is a measure of the total supply of goods and services produced in the economy during a year.

The total demand for goods and services is made up of total spending by consumers, businesses in the form of investment, and all levels of government.[2] If the total of consumption spending, plus investment spending, plus

---

[2]Some of our output is sold to foreign nations in the form of exports. However, since exports are roughly offset by an equal volume of imports, we shall ignore this source of demand.

government spending, is equal to GNP, the economy is in equilibrium. In other words, when total demand (C + I + G) equals total supply (GNP), there is no tendency for the total production to either increase or decrease. The GNP will tend to remain constant.

However, if the total demand (C + I + G) is less than the total supply (GNP), there will tend to be a decrease in the GNP. For example, suppose the GNP is $900 billion. If the total spending by consumers, business units, and government is only $850 billion, total supply (GNP) exceeds total demand (C + I + G) by $50 billion. Inventories will build up and producers will begin to reduce production and lay off workers. Thus, when total demand is less than the total supply of goods and services, unemployment will tend to result.

Suppose, on the other hand, that the total demand (C + I + G) is $950 billion and the GNP is $900 billion. The total demand exceeds the total supply by $50 billion. If the economy is not operating at full-employment capacity, production may increase by $50 billion to eliminate the shortage and bring total supply and total demand into balance.

However, suppose that the $900 billion GNP is the maximum which the economy can produce at this time. In other words, the economy is operating at the full-employment level. With a full-employment GNP of $900 billion and a total demand of $950 billion, a shortage will result. The shortage will cause buyers to compete for the short supply of goods and services, and prices will be bid up. Ultimately, the $900 billion worth of physical goods and services will tend to sell for a total of $950 billion, because of the increased prices. Since the GNP is defined as the *dollar value* of goods and services produced in a year's time measured in terms of their market prices, the GNP will rise by $50 billion even though the physical volume of goods and services produced will remain unchanged. This is "demand-pull" inflation. Statisticians will use price indices to adjust the GNP to constant dollars (based on prices of a previous year). However, it will be reported both in terms of current dollars and constant dollars.

In conclusion, any time the total demand (C + I + G) exceeds the GNP, the GNP will tend to rise. If the economy has unemployed resources available to increase total production, real GNP will rise. If, however, the economy is already operating at the full-employment maximum-production level, the increase in GNP will result only in higher prices, with the physical volume of goods and services remaining unchanged. Therefore, at times of full employment, it is extremely important that policies be aimed at discouraging any increase in total spending.

Excess-Demand Inflation Without Excess Demand for the Entire Economy

"Demand-pull" inflation is generally associated with the problem of excess demand for the economy as a whole. In the past it was often asserted that excess-demand inflation could not take place so long as unemployment existed. The presence of unemployed resources indicated that the output of the economy (GNP) was below its full capacity. Therefore, if the total demand (C + I + G) exceeded the GNP, the physical output of the economy should increase rather than prices.

The experiences of recent years indicate that substantial inflation can occur during periods of considerable unemployment. Some of this inflation can be attributed to the fact that powerful business enterprises and unions may arbitrarily raise their prices and wages above the level that would prevail if greater competition existed. This is "administered-price" inflation and will be discussed later.

However, not all of the inflation during periods of unemployment can be attributed to administered prices. From March 1973 to March 1974, average consumer prices rose by 10.2 percent. During the same twelve-month period average food prices rose by 18.3 percent. Since agriculture is one of the most competitive industries in the United States, the above average price increases for food cannot be attributed to "administered-price" inflation. Farmers are unable to dictate the prices that they receive. Prices are determined by supply and demand in the market. Thus, the increased food prices were primarily. the result of excess demand for food. This came at a time when there was substantial unemployment in the economy.

At the same time that there were shortages of food, oil, and other items, there were undoubtedly surpluses of some other things. However, while a shortage almost always means a price increase, a surplus does not necessarily mean a price decrease. Prices often tend to be inflexible downward in our economy. Thus, the increased prices resulting from excess demand in some markets may not be offset by decreasing prices in those areas where surpluses exist. When demand increases, prices rise. When demand declines, prices often remain stable instead of declining. How often does one hear about workers negotiating the size of a wage cut because the demand for their labor has declined? Similarly, one would not expect the auto makers to announce a price reduction simply because sales are off. Hence, while prices do move up and down in certain competitive industries such as agriculture, for many items in our economy the direction of the price change is always upward.

The important point is that excess-demand inflation can occur even when the economy is operating below full employment. The name given to this inflation is not so important as the recognition of the cause of the higher prices. Many economists are reluctant to call it "demand-pull" inflation since this term has traditionally been applied to a situation where the economy is operating at full capacity. Often it is called "structural" inflation because it is at least partly caused by structural problems in the economy which do not permit the quick transfer of surplus unemployed resources to other areas where shortages exist. For example, there may be a surplus of automobiles and a shortage of gasoline. However, the surplus equipment in the automobile factories cannot be readily converted to oil drilling and refining equipment.

Regardless of the name applied to it, the type of inflation we have been discussing in this section is caused by excess demand. In other words, the quantity demanded exceeds the available supply. When there is not enough of an item to supply all potential buyers at the existing prices, there will have to be a price increase in order to equate supply and demand. To the extent that rising prices for certain items whose demand has increased are not offset by declining prices for other items, excess-demand inflation will occur even though the economy may be operating below the full-employment level.

Administered-Price Inflation

"Administered-price" inflation occurs when prices are arbitrarily increased by sellers even though there may be no increase in demand for the items in question. The administered price increase may be motivated by a rise in production costs such as a wage increase. It may also be motivated by a desire to increase profits or a desire to avoid a profit reduction which might result from an anticipated future wage increase.

"Administered-price" inflation includes what is generally referred to as "cost-push" and "profit-push" inflation. "Cost-push" inflation occurs when production his prices in order to compensate for the increased wage costs and thus avoid a reduction in profit. "Profit-push" inflation occurs when producers raise prices in order to increase profit margins, even before wages have gone up. In both cases, the inflation results from administered price increases which may occur even though there is no shortage of the products in question.

Competition and Administered-Price Inflation

"Administered-price" inflation can exist only under certain market situations. The greater the degree of competition, the more difficult it is for sellers to engage in "administered-price" inflation. It is virtually impossible for a single small farmer to have any control over the price of his grain. If when farmer Jones takes his wheat to the market place the price is $3.00 per bushel, he has only two options. He must take the market price or keep his wheat. If he says I will sell my wheat for $3.30 per bushel, he will be unable to sell any of his wheat. He can hold on to his wheat and hope that the forces of supply and demand will dictate a higher price at some future date. However, if he wants to sell his wheat on that day, he must accept the going market price which has been determined by supply and demand forces.

Most businessmen in today's economy are not confronted with the same grim "take it or leave it" reality which farmer Jones faces. In most cases a businessman can increase his price within reasonable limits and still have a substantial volume of sales. Usually, his sales will decline somewhat when he raises his price, but will not go to zero as is the case with farmer Jones. For example, if General Motors decides to raise the list price on one of its models from $4,000 to $4,400, it may experience some decline in sales, but will still be able to sell a substantial number of automobiles at the new price. Yet, when farmer Jones attempts to raise his price by the same 10 percent he finds that he can sell none of his wheat. The greater the competition, the less control the businessman has over the price of his product.

Elasticity of Demand and Administered-Price Inflation

The amount by which a seller is able to increase his price without adversely affecting his sales is determined by what economists call price elasticity of demand. Price elasticity of demand is a measure of the responsiveness of quantity demanded to a change in price. If a small price increase will bring about a large reduction in sales, the product is said to have a highly elastic demand and the seller is effectively barred from initiating irresponsibly large price increases. On the other hand, if a relatively large price increase will have little or no effect on sales, the product has an inelastic demand and the seller is in a position to exploit his customers if he so desires.

Many factors affect the elasticity of demand for a particular seller's product. However, the most important factors are (1) the number of other sellers, (2) whether or not the product is considered a necessity by consumers, and (3) whether or not good substitutes are available.

The number of other sellers in the market area is a crucial factor in determining the degree to which a seller can engage in administered-price inflation. If a traveler finds himself in a remote town with one gas station, he may have to pay an exorbitant price for gas unless he has enough left in his tank to get to the next town. The single gas station owner is free to raise his price at will in the absence of any government controls. However, in a town with a substantial number of competing gas stations an individual station owner will find that he has far less freedom to raise prices at will. If he sets his price ten cents per gallon higher than most of the other stations in town he will lose most of his customers, assuming of course that the customers are aware of the price difference. Thus, the demand facing a single seller of gasoline in a remote town might be quite inelastic, while the demand facing an individual station owner in a city with many competing stations might be very elastic.

The degree to which consumers consider a product a necessity is very important in determining the elasticity of demand. A diabetic must have his daily dose of insulin in order to stay alive. If the price were to double, or triple, he would still buy the same amount. If the price were to increase tenfold, the diabetic would still buy the same amount of insulin so long as he had sufficient money to pay for it. If a single company were to obtain exclusive control of the production of insulin, or any other essential drug, it would be in a position to exploit those individuals who must have the drug to live. Therefore, it is extremely important that either strong competition, or government regulation, prevail in such areas. While few products may be as necessary to the consumer as life-maintaining drugs, many products are urgently needed. For the individual who lives some distance from his job in an area where no public transportation exists, gasoline to get to work becomes an absolute necessity. Fuel to heat one's home is another example of a product which is absolutely essential. Many items are considered by consumers to be very essential, while other items are generally considered to be luxuries.

If an item is generally considered to be a necessity, the demand for the product will be inelastic. In other words, consumers will continue to buy about the same amounts of the product even after substantial price increases. On the other hand, if the item is generally considered to be a luxury, price increases will usually result in substantial reductions in sales.

The availability of good substitutes will usually increase the elasticity of demand for a product. For example, while many people consider meat a necessity, few individuals would consider pork, or beef, a necessity. While most individuals have their preferences, pork and beef are generally considered substitutable for each other. If the price of beef were suddenly to double, many beef consumers would switch to pork and there would be a substantial reduction in beef sales. Also, if the price of natural gas were to increase substantially relative to other heating fuels, many homeowners would probably switch to oil or electric heat.

In conclusion, the elasticity of demand for a product is influenced by many factors. If a single seller were to have exclusive control of an absolute necessity for which there were no satisfactory substitutes, he would have very great exploitative powers. Fortunately, it would probably be impossible to attain such a position in our economy. However, many sellers do have a considerable amount of market power and are able to have considerable control over the prices they receive for their products. If this were not so, "administered-price" inflation would not be a problem.

Summary

1. Several descriptive terms have been coined to refer to different types of inflation. Terms such as "hyperinflation," "runaway inflation," "galloping infla-tion," "creeping inflation," "walking inflation," and "trot-ting inflation" refer to different rates of inflation. Terms such as "demand-pull," "cost-push," "wage-push," "profit-push," "administered-price," and "structural" in-flation are used to describe inflation in terms of the underlying causes.

2. Despite the many descriptive terms applied to inflation, there are two basic underlying causes of inflation. Inflation is caused by excess demand, and by the activities of unions and businessmen where competition is insufficient to prevent administered wage and price increases.

3. If the demand for an item exceeds the available supply, the price will tend to rise. Rising prices serve as a rationing device and also may encourage additional production of the scarce items. If the total demand for all goods and services produced in the economy exceeds the productive capacity of the economy, general "demand-pull" inflation will occur. It is possible to have inflation which is caused by excess demand for some items even though the economy is not operating at maximum capacity.

4. "Administered-price" inflation occurs when prices are arbitrarily increased by sellers even though there may be no increase in demand for the items in question. The greater the degree of competition, the more difficult it is for sellers to engage in "administered-price" inflation.

5. Price elasticity of demand is a measure of the responsiveness of quantity demanded to a change in price. The more elastic the demand, the greater the reduction in sales from a given price increase. The number of other sellers, whether or not the product is a necessity, and whether or not good substitutes are available are all important determinants of the elasticity of demand facing an individual seller.

6. Price elasticity of demand is an important determinant of the degree to which sellers can engage in "administered-price" inflation. If a single seller were to have exclusive control of an absolute necessity for which there were no satisfactory substitutes, he would have very great exploitative powers. While no seller could ever attain such an extreme position, many sellers do have considerable control over the prices they receive.

3   Types of Unemployment & Causes

In the minds of most people there is probably only one type of unemployment. It usually means no work and no pay. Certainly, the unemployed worker does not care what label is placed on his joblessness. He simply wants to return to work and resume his role as provider for his family.

However, not all unemployment is the same in terms of causation. The effect on the jobless worker is probably the same regardless of the cause of his unemployment, but policies aimed at correcting the unemployment problem must recognize the different causal factors. In this chapter we will examine the various types of unemployment and the causes of each.

Measurement of Unemployment

A first step in understanding unemployment is an

understanding of how the unemployment statistics are obtained, and what the statistics mean. Each month the Bureau of the Census conducts a survey for the Department of Labor to determine the size of the labor force, the number of persons employed, and the number of persons unemployed. The survey is based on a probability sample of about 47,000 households. The individuals surveyed are asked a series of questions aimed at determining whether or not they are in the labor force, and if so, whether or not they are employed. Those individuals classified as in the labor force and employed are those who are actively working plus those with a job who are temporarily absent because of vacations, illness, labor disputes or bad weather.

Those classified as in the labor force and unemployed are those persons who had no employment during the survey week and were actively seeking employment. In order for the individual to be placed in this category he must have engaged in specific job seeking activity within the past four weeks, or be waiting to be called back to a job from which he has been laid off, or be waiting to report to a new job within the following thirty days. An individual who is not working and is not actively seeking work because he has become discouraged and believes no jobs are available is not classified as unemployed. Such an individual is simply excluded from the labor force count.

Shortcomings of the Unemployment Statistics

There are several shortcomings to the official labor force and unemployment statistics. First of all, the labor force statistics do not indicate the total potential manpower available to the economy. The official labor force includes only those persons in the noninstitutional population (excludes inmates of prisons, etc.), sixteen years of age and over, who are currently working or are actively seeking work. It excludes persons under sixteen years of age although some persons below that age are working. There is probably a considerable hidden manpower potential in the non-labor force population. It is not known how many students and housewives would enter the labor force if good jobs were suddenly to become plentiful. The unemployment statistics exclude not only many nonworking individuals who might work if jobs were plentiful, but also those working individuals who are working part-time. If a man who has lost his regular forty hours per week job finds employment for half a day per week as a Saturday afternoon gasoline station attendant, he is removed from the unemployed classification and classified as employed. Even a person who has worked as little as one hour for pay during the survey week is counted as employed rather than unemployed. This causes a distortion in the unemployment statistics. During periods of declining employment many workers will be reduced to part-time employment. This reduction in employment will not show up in the unemployment figures.

Types of Unemployment

Economists generally divide unemployment into three categories based on the causal factors. These categories are frictional unemployment, cyclical unemployment, and structural unemployment. A fourth category, seasonal fluctuations, is also often included.

Frictional Unemployment

Full employment does not mean zero unemployment. In a dynamic economy such as ours it would be impossible to attain zero unemployment. Furthermore, it would be undesirable. It would mean that no employee could ever quit his job and no employer could ever dismiss an employee.

At any point in time a substantial number of people have just quit their job, have just been fired, or have just left school and are seeking employment for the first time. One month later many of these people will have found employment, but a new group of individuals will have just left their jobs. This type of unemployment is known as frictional unemployment. It involves individuals who are between jobs.

A certain amount of frictional unemployment is necessary to provide freedom and mobility to workers. However, there is considerable disagreement as to how much frictional unemployment is necessary. The estimates usually range from 3 percent to 5 percent of the labor force. Most experts consider 4 percent unemployment to be full employment. However, some economists believe that with the correct policies frictional unemployment could be reduced considerably below the 4 percent level.

A difference of 1 percent in the unemployment rate is quite significant. The total civilian labor force for January 1975 was 92,091,000 persons. With a 1 percent reduction in unemployment, 920,910 more individuals would have had jobs. Therefore, it makes a considerable difference to many individuals whether the government shoots for a full employment target of 3 percent, 4 percent, or 5 percent unemployment. Methods of reducing frictional unemployment will be discussed in Chapter 7.

Cyclical Unemployment

Throughout the history of the American economy the major kind of unemployment has been cyclical. Cyclical unemployment results from business recessions and depressions when total spending is below the full-employment productive capacity of the economy.

During the great depression of the 1930s, nearly 25 percent of the labor force was unemployed. This was not because the nation had suddenly become impoverished in terms of resources. The economy had basically the same abundance of natural resources, manpower, and productive equipment which it had before the depression. In other words, the economy had basically the same capacity to produce the abundance of goods and services that it was producing before the depression. Why then did the economy not continue to produce at the full-employment level? The total answer is rather complex, but basically, the economy did not produce because the goods and services being produced were not being purchased. The economic system simply broke down. People lost their jobs because people were not buying. People were not buying because they either had lost their jobs or feared the loss of their jobs.

The Importance of the Total Spending Level. While we are not likely ever again to experience the degree of cyclical unemployment which plagued the economy during the 1930s, cyclical unemployment of a lesser degree has continued to be a persistent problem facing the American economy. The cause of cyclical unemployment is very simple. The solution is very complex. The economy will not continue to produce at the full-employment level unless the total output is purchased. No businessman could continue producing a fixed quantity of output per month indefinitely if only 90 percent of the output was being purchased. As his inventories accumulated he would eventually have to curtail his production and lay off some of his workers. The same is true for the economy as a whole. If the economy is capable of producing $950 billion worth of goods and services per year at full employment, there will have to be $950 billion worth of purchases per year in order for the economy to continue to operate at full capacity. If total spending declines, then total production will also decline and workers will lose their jobs. Of course, the productive capacity of the economy is continually growing because of technological advance and other factors. Therefore, it will be necessary for total spending to increase at the same rate if unemployment is to be avoided.

Components of Aggregate Demand.   When we say that total spending must equal total production in order to maintain full employment, we are not referring to the spending of consumers alone. It would be foolhardy for a nation to completely consume its total output each year. Consumer spending is only one component of total demand for the economy. The total demand for the economy as a whole is made up of the spending of consumers, all units of government, and businessmen in the form of investment.

Investment, in the economic sense, refers to such things as the building of new factories, machines, etc. The building of some new factories and machines is necessary just to offset the wearing out of old factories and machines. However, the economy usually engages in more investment than is necessary to replace capital equipment which is wearing out. Thus, part of the investment spending is for expansion of the productive capacity of the economy.

The Savings Equal Investment Problem.   Where do the funds for investment spending come from? Part comes from business savings. However, a substantial amount of business investment is financed by the savings of households. Hence, it is not necessary for each individual to spend his entire income each year in order for the economy to remain at full employment. On the contrary, individual savings provide funds for the expansion of the productive capacity of the economy so that we can all enjoy a higher standard of living in the future.

The problem comes when the amount of total savings is not completely offset by an equal amount of investment. To the extent that investment spending falls short of the amount of savings, there will tend to be a contraction in the economy, and unemployment will tend to result, assuming that government spending remains unchanged.

While it is extremely important that savings equal investment, it is highly unlikely that the two will be equal. Saving and investment are done by different groups of people and for different reasons. Households save for a variety of reasons: to purchase a new car or home; to provide for future security during the retirement years; to provide a college education for their children; or to amass an estate to pass on to their children.

Businessmen invest on the basis of profit expectations. The number of highly profitable investment opportunities available to businessmen fluctuates considerably from year to year. The development of new industries such as the automobile or plastics industries provided tremendous opportunities for new investment. The opening of new frontiers in the past also provided abundant opportunities for investment. However, in a highly developed economy such as ours, few new frontiers are opened, and the development of new products and new industries is very sporadic. Therefore, the amount of investment from year to year tends to be highly variable and is not likely to be equal to the amount of savings. Thus, without government intervention the economy is likely to suffer fluctuations in production and employment. This is due largely to fluctuations in investment but can also be caused by fluctuations in consumption and government spending.

The C + I + G = Full-Employment GNP Requirement. The key to maintaining full employment in the economy is the maintenance of a total spending level equal to the full-employment productive capacity of the economy. Since investment tends to fluctuate considerably, total spending cannot be held at

the full-employment level without government intervention. When investment falls, actions should be taken
either to increase investment or to provide offsetting
increases in consumption spending and/or government
spending. In other words, when total spending (aggregate
demand) falls short of total output (GNP), balance can be
restored by increasing any or all of the three basic
components of aggregate demand. Since aggregate
demand is made up of consumption spending (C), plus
investment spending (I), plus government spending (G),
full-employment stability requires the following
condition:

$$C + I + G = \text{Full-Employment GNP}$$

Consumption spending, plus investment spending,
plus government spending, must equal the full-
employment GNP if the economy is to remain at the full-
employment output. The specific amount of consumption, investment, or government spending is not nearly as
important as the combined total of all three. Three
combinations of aggregate demand which add up to the
correct amount for maintaining full employment are
given below.

C ($610B) + I ($130B) + G ($210B) =
Full-Employment GNP ($950B)
C ($600B) + I ($150B) + G ($200B) =
Full-Employment GNP ($950B)
C ($620B) + I ($110B) + G ($220B) =
Full-Employment GNP ($950B)

Assuming that the economy has a full-employment
productive capacity of $950 billion, any of the above
combinations would be sufficient to maintain full
employment. You will note that the individual amounts
of consumption spending, investment spending, and
government spending are different in each of the three
examples. However the total of C + I + G is $950 billion in

each case, which is just the exact amount needed to balance the full-employment GNP of $950 billion.

The goal is to maintain a total spending level equal to the full-employment GNP. If investment spending declines by $10 billion, but is offset by a $10 billion increase in consumption or government spending, the total spending level can still be maintained at the proper level.

Our discussion thus far in this chapter has been restricted to the problem of keeping the total spending level from falling below the full-employment GNP. This is only half of the problem. It is equally important to prevent the total spending level from climbing above the full-employment GNP. If the aggregate demand (C + I + G) exceeds the full-employment level of output, demand-pull inflation will occur. Thus, if total spending is too low, unemployment will result. If it is too high, inflation will occur.

The Feasibility of Maintaining Proper Aggregate Demand. Maintaining aggregate demand at exactly the proper level to avoid both inflation and unemployment is impossible with our present knowledge of the economy. In fact, there is no exact level of aggregate demand which would avoid both unemployment and inflation. There is really no exact point which we can refer to as the full-employment level. Instead, there is a high-employment zone ranging from perhaps 3 percent to 5 percent unemployment, toward which the economy can be moved. The farther the economy is moved into the high employment zone, the greater the inflationary pressures. Therefore, most experts believe that a well-managed economy will have both some unemployment and some inflation. However, it should be possible to keep both of these undesirable conditions to a minimum. Accomplishing this goal involves manipulation of the basic components of aggregate demand (C + I + G). Techniques of manipulating aggregate demand will be discussed in later chapters.

Structural Unemployment

Structural unemployment involves a mismatch between job seekers and job openings. It can occur when the level of aggregate demand is relatively high and a substantial number of job openings are available. It occurs because the job seekers are in some way prevented from filling the job vacancies. Usually structural unemployment results from either a geographic mismatch or a skill mismatch.

Geographic Mismatch.   A geographic mismatch occurs when there are unfilled job vacancies in one geographic area and unemployed workers who are qualified to fill the vacancies in another geographic area. The jobs will not move to the unemployed workers, and many of the unemployed workers will not move to the jobs.

The coal mining regions of Appalachia provide an excellent example of structural unemployment caused by a geographic mismatch. Many of the unemployed workers in this region are former coal miners or the children of coal miners. Because of the exhaustion of coal deposits in some areas and the extensive application of technology in the mining process, many jobs have been eliminated. As a result, many workers find themselves without jobs in an area where there are few alternative sources of employment. The solution to this unemployment problem must involve either a movement of unemployed workers out of the region to other areas where job vacancies exist or an inflow of new industries into the high unemployment areas. Both of these potential solutions involve complex problems.

Many of the unemployed workers have deep roots in

the region and have had little or no contact with the outside world. A movement from a rural region in Appalachia which has always been home, to an urban center where employment prospects may be greater, would be a very traumatic experience for many workers. Many unemployed workers in Appalachia have such deep roots in their local area that they prefer to suffer the consequences of unemployment and poverty at home rather than move to a new and unfamiliar area in hopes of improving their economic status.

The problem of encouraging new industries to move into the depressed areas is also a difficult one. Many areas are isolated and do not have sufficient highways, airports, water resources, and the like to attract new industries. In many areas, public facilities will have to be substantially upgraded in order to attract potential new employers. Even then, it may be difficult to persuade businessmen to locate their new production units in these areas when they are being wooed by communities throughout the nation.

Skill Mismatch. A skill mismatch occurs when there are both job vacancies and unemployed job seekers in the same geographic area, but the job seekers are not qualified to fill the vacancies. In the past, this problem was thought to result largely from the fact that most of the job vacancies required considerable skill and education, and most of the unemployed were unskilled and undereducated. A potential solution to the problem appeared to be a general upgrading in the educational and skill levels of the population as a whole. However, in recent years it has become increasingly apparent that more than a general increase in the educational level of the work force is necessary. It is also important that new entrants into the labor force have their training in those fields where employment is expanding. In other words, it is possible to have job vacancies requiring a high skill level in the same geographic area where there is a substantial number of highly educated unemployed workers. For example, today there is a surplus of young people trained as school teachers. At the same time, many occupations requiring four years of college training have a shortage of personnel. The school teachers have four years of college training, but their training is not in the proper fields to qualify them for employment in those areas where job vacancies exist. Thus, a skill mismatch may involve highly skilled job vacancies and unskilled undereducated applicants, or it may involve a situation where the job applicants are highly educated but in the wrong fields to qualify them for employment in the job openings. Basically, the solution to the problem involves better supply and demand projections for various occupations and an improved counseling program which would communicate this information to young people before they begin their career training.

Seasonal Fluctuations

Seasonal fluctuations in employment are a problem in some industries. Agricultural workers will alternate between periods of peak employment during the harvest seasons and other periods of high unemployment. Construction workers are adversely affected by inclement weather. Employees in tourist resorts will often not be fully employed for the entire year. Also, many manufacturing firms produce products which have a seasonal market. Therefore, at any point in time some of the unemployment in the economy involves workers who normally have work, but are temporarily unemployed due to seasonal factors. A certain amount of seasonal unemployment is unavoidable. However, with better work scheduling seasonal fluctuations can be reduced in some industries.

Underemployment

Workers are classified as unemployed only if they are

not working at all. However, many workers who would like to have full-time employment are working only part time. Other workers, who are working at full-time jobs, are employed in jobs substantially below their educational and skill levels.

A worker is considered underemployed if: (1) he is working only part time and would like to have a full-time job; (2) he is working at a job below his skill and educational level. An accountant working as a gasoline station attendant is underemployed. A measure can be obtained for those individuals who are working only part-time. However, it would be impossible to obtain an objective measure of those who are working below their skill level. Whether or not a worker is qualified for a higher level job than he now is performing often involves a subjective judgment. However, there is little doubt that many employees in our economy are working at jobs which are below their present or potential capabilities. This constitutes underemployment.

Summary

1. The employment, unemployment, and labor force statistics are collected for the Department of Labor by the Bureau of the Census in a monthly survey of some 47,000 households. The unemployment statistics exclude many nonworking individuals who might work if jobs were plentiful, and those individuals who are working only part time.

2. Economists generally divide unemployment into three categories based on causal factors. These categories are frictional unemployment, cyclical unemployment, and structural unemployment. A fourth category, seasonal fluctuations, is also often included.

3. Frictional unemployment involves individuals who are between jobs. Since a certain amount of frictional unemployment is unavoidable, full employment does not mean zero unemployment. Full employment is usually

defined as somewhere between 3 percent and 5 percent unemployment.

4. Cyclical unemployment results from business recessions and depressions when the total spending in the economy is below the full-employment productive capacity. The aggregate demand for the economy consists of the total spending of consumers, all units of government, and businesses in the form of investment. For full employment to exist, the aggregate demand must equal the full-employment GNP of the economy.

5. Structural unemployment involves a mismatch between job seekers and job openings. It can result from either a geographic or a skill mismatch.

6. Seasonal fluctuations in employment are a problem in certain industries such as agriculture and the construction industry. At any point in time some of the unemployment in the economy involves workers who normally have work but are temporarily unemployed due to seasonal factors.

7. Many employed workers are underemployed. A worker is underemployed if he is working only part time and would like to have a full-time job, or if he is working at a job below his skill and educational level.

4 The Role of the Federal Reserve System & Monetary Policy in Controlling Inflation & Unemployment

In Chapter 1 we discussed the difficulty of reaching agreement on what combination of inflation and unemployment public policy should be aimed at. However, the problem of setting the policy goal is small compared to the problem of attaining it. Steering the economy between the extremes of high inflation and high unemployment is a very difficult feat. However, it is not an impossible one. Although the steering mechanism of the economy is a very crude one, there are devices available to the policy makers which can be used to prevent the economy from straying too far from the desired course. The most important tools for controlling the economy can be divided into two general categories, monetary policy tools and fiscal policy tools. Monetary policy involves changes in the availability and cost of credit. Fiscal policy involves changes in government spending and taxing policies. We will examine monetary policy in depth later in this chapter, and fiscal policy will be covered in the next chapter.

The Federal Reserve System

In order to understand monetary policy it is important to have at least a cursory knowledge of the American banking system. Since monetary policy is conducted by the top authorities of the Federal Reserve System, we will briefly examine the organization of the Federal Reserve System before proceeding to monetary policy.

Unlike most other advanced countries which have a single central bank, the United States has twelve. At the time the Federal Reserve System was being created there was a fear of a totally centralized American banking system. Also, when the possibility of having a single central bank was considered, there was considerable disagreement over where it should be located. Western farmers feared that a central bank located in the East would not be familiar with and responsive to their financial needs. Eastern businessmen had similar fears about a central bank located in the West.

The Federal Reserve System was a compromise between those who wanted centralization and those who favored decentralization. Instead of creating a single central bank, the Federal Reserve Act divided the nation into twelve districts and established a Federal Reserve Bank to serve as a central bank in each district.

However, the twelve Federal Reserve Banks are centrally controlled by the Board of Governors. The Board of Governors of the Federal Reserve System is the top authority of our money and banking system. The seven members of the Board are appointed by the President, with the confirmation of the Senate, for fourteen-year terms. The terms are staggered so that one member is replaced every two years. Board members are appointed rather than elected, in an attempt to keep partisan politics out of monetary policy. Also, the long and staggered terms tend to provide the Board with continuity and experienced membership.

The Board of Governors is responsible for the general supervision and control of the money and banking system of the nation. The Board's actions determine the basic policies which the commercial banking system is to follow. The actions of the Board are to be in the public interest and designed to promote the general economic welfare.

Two important bodies assist the Board of Governors in determining basic policies. The Federal Open Market Committee, which consists of the seven members of the Board of Governors plus five of the presidents of Federal Reserve Banks, determines the System's policy with regard to the purchase and sale of government securities in the open market. These open-market operations constitute the most effective monetary policy tool available to the monetary authorities and will be more thoroughly discussed later in this chapter.

The other body which assists the Board is the Federal Advisory Council, which is made up of twelve prominent commercial bankers. One member of the council is selected by each of the twelve Federal Reserve Banks. The Council meets with the Board of Governors periodically to express its views on banking policy.

The Federal Reserve Banks are privately owned but governmentally controlled. They are quasi-public banks. When commercial banks join the Federal Reserve System they are required to purchase shares of stock in the Federal Reserve Bank in their district. Thus, each of the twelve Federal Reserve Banks is owned by the member banks in that district. However, the basic policies which the Federal Reserve Banks pursue are established by the Board of Governors, a government body.

The Federal Reserve Banks are frequently referred to as "bankers' banks" since they perform essentially the same functions for commercial banks that commercial banks perform for the public. The Federal Reserve Banks normally do not deal with the public. Generally they deal exclusively with the government and the commercial banks. A very important function of the Federal Reserve Banks is the issuance of currency. The Federal Reserve Banks have been authorized by Congress to issue Federal Reserve Notes. These Federal Reserve Notes constitute the nation's paper money.

The Money Supply

The money supply of the economy is generally defined as the total currency in circulation (paper money and coins outside of banks) plus demand deposits (checking accounts). While most economists would agree with this definition, they are not all satisfied with it. Some economists believe that time deposits (savings accounts) in commercial banks should also be included in the money supply. However, the official definition of the money supply for the United States includes only coins and paper currency in circulation, plus demand deposits.

Money is usually defined as anything which is generally acceptable in exchange and is generally used for payment. Coins and paper currency in circulation certainly fit this definition. Not only are coins and paper currency generally acceptable in exchange, but they are also legal tender. This means that they must be accepted as payment for any debt, public or private.

Demand deposits (checking accounts) do not have legal-tender status. Thus, a creditor could legally refuse to accept your personal check without canceling your debt to him. However, since checks are generally acceptable in exchange and generally used for payments, they are money. A demand deposit constitutes a promise on the part of a bank to pay immediately the amount of money specified by the customer who owns the demand deposit. In other words, when you deposit cash in your checking account, that cash becomes payable on demand to you or anyone else to whom you write a check. It is "checkbook money." You can generally pay your bills with it, and you can usually spend it in most local stores simply by writing checks for the items you buy. Demand deposits constitute nearly 80 percent of the money supply. The remainder is made up of coins and paper money.

Time deposits (savings accounts) are different from demand deposits in two important respects. First, you cannot pay a bill with your savings account passbook. You must instead go to the bank and withdraw cash from your account. When you do this the currency in circulation has increased and the cash becomes part of the money supply.

The second important difference between time deposits and demand deposits is that time deposits are not payable on demand. When you go to the bank to withdraw cash from your savings account, the bank can legally refuse to give you the cash at that time. Instead, they may require you to give sixty days' written notice before you can receive your money. While banks seldom exercise this option on small withdrawals, they do have the right to do so. Thus, time deposits are excluded from the money supply.

Changes in the Money Supply

The money supply of the economy is not an unchanging constant amount. In fact, the money supply is constantly changing for a variety of reasons. Therefore, even if the monetary authorities deemed it desirable to maintain a relatively constant money supply they would have to take action in order to accomplish that goal.

Actually, most authorities believe that the money supply should be increased at times and decreased at other times in an effort to influence economic activity. Thus, the monetary authorities deliberately change the money supply in order to bring it nearer to the level they believe desirable. Changes in the money supply are brought about primarily through open-market operations, which we shall discuss shortly.

The Money Supply and Prices

There is obviously a relationship between the money supply and the price level. If we were suddenly to have a doubling in the money supply, prices would certainly increase. When people possess twice as much money as before, they will increase their spending in an effort to buy more goods and services. However, since there are no more goods and services than before, the only result can be higher prices. That prices would increase if the money supply doubled is beyond question. However, we cannot be sure that prices would exactly double. While there is definitely a relationship between the money supply and prices, it is not a precise predictable relationship.

Early economists, who believed that there was a precise relationship between the money supply and prices, originated the "quantity theory of money." In its crudest form, this theory argues that the level of prices in the economy is directly proportional to the quantity of money in circulation. In other words, a given percentage change in the money supply would cause an equal percentage change in the price level. For example, a 10 percent increase in the money supply would cause a 10 percent increase in the price level, and a 10 percent decrease in the money supply would cause a 10 percent decline in prices.

If the quantity theory of money were valid, curing

inflation would be a simple task. Unfortunately, the theory does not work out in practice.

Instruments of Monetary Policy

The objective of monetary policy is to influence aggregate demand (C + I + G) and move it nearer to the level required for maintaining full employment with relatively stable prices. The technique by which the policy makers attempt to accomplish this objective is to influence the cost and availability of credit.

In addition to earned income as a source of spendable funds, borrowed money plays a very important role in our economy. Not only do consumers and businessmen engage in credit buying, but also governments through the sale of bonds partially operate on borrowed money. It is on credit buying that monetary policy has its effect. The primary impact of monetary policy is on investment spending, but there is also some effect on consumption spending, and probably some effect on spending by local units of government. There are basically three important tools available to the Federal Reserve authorities which can be used to influence the availability and cost of credit, and thus the level of total spending. These tools are: (1) changes in reserve requirements, (2) open-market operations, and (3) changes in the discount rate. Two additional minor tools available to the monetary authorities are moral suasion and margin regulations on the purchase of stock.

Changes in Reserve Requirements

Commercial banks are required by law to hold a certain minimum percentage of their deposits as reserves. These reserves may be held as deposits with a Federal Reserve Bank or as cash in the vault. Neither cash in the vault nor deposits in the Federal Reserve Bank earn interest. Therefore, most commercial banks will not maintain reserves substantially above the minimum required by law. Any reserves above and beyond those required by law are "free reserves" and can be invested or loaned out.

The legal reserve requirement depends on both the size of the bank and the policy of the Fed.[3] Generally the larger the deposits of a bank, the higher the reserve requirement. Also, the Fed has the authority to change the reserve requirements within established legal limits.

Suppose a bank has a 10 percent reserve requirement, and you deposit $1000 in your checking account. The bank is required to keep $100 of your money as a reserve and can lend the other $900 out, assuming that it was just meeting its legal reserve requirement before your deposit. Now suppose that Mr. B borrows the $900 and uses it to purchase something from Mr. C. Mr. C then deposits the $900 in his bank. His bank must set aside 10 percent ($90) as a reserve for his deposit and may lend the other $810. This chain of events could conceivably continue through many more steps, ultimately increasing the total money supply by as much as $9000.

This is known as multiple expansion of bank deposits through the banking system. It is not important for the general reader to understand the mechanics of this multiple expansion process. The important point is that, while a single commercial bank can lend only the amount of its "free reserves" (actual reserves minus required reserves), the banking system as a whole can expand the money supply by a multiple of this amount. When the banking system receives new reserves, it can expand the total money supply by a multiple of these new reserves. Furthermore, the smaller the legal reserve requirement, the greater the potential expansion in the money supply from any given increase in reserves. Since the Federal Reserve authorities have the power to change both the

---

[3]The Federal Reserve System is generally referred to as the "Fed."

amount of reserves held by commercial banks and the legal reserve requirement, within limits, they have considerable control over the money supply of the nation.

Open-Market Operations

Because of the large federal debt in this country, U.S. government bonds are owned by a large variety of individuals and organizations including the Federal Reserve Banks and commercial banks. Most of these bonds are of short-term maturity and can be bought and sold at any time from date of issuance to date of maturity. These are not the long-term maturity savings bonds which usually come to mind when one talks about government bonds. Only a very small fraction of the federal debt consists of the common savings bonds. Most of the debt is in the form of reasonably high-yielding short-term securities which are bought and sold by investors.

There is an organized market for these government securities very similar to the stock exchange. Investors can buy and sell on a daily basis very much as they would buy and sell stocks. Since the Federal Reserve Banks own a substantial volume of government securities, they can sell on the open market if they choose to do so, or they can buy additional securities.

Open-market operations consist of the buying and selling of government securities in the open market by the Federal Reserve authorities. Through open-market operations the Fed pumps money into or out of the economy. When the Fed sells bonds the purchasers must pay for these bonds, thus reducing the money supply and/or the potential expansion of the money supply. If members of the nonbank public buy the bonds, they will write checks on their accounts, thus reducing the volume of demand deposits in the economy. This constitutes a direct reduction in the money supply since demand deposits are part of the money supply. Furthermore, when the checks come back to the commercial banks for clearance the banks lose reserves, thus reducing the potential for an expansion in the money supply. If the bonds which the Fed sells are purchased by commercial banks, which is often the case, the commercial banks will pay for the bonds with free reserves, again reducing the potential for an expansion of the money supply.

When the Fed buys bonds, it pays the sellers, thus increasing the money supply and/or the potential expansion of the money supply. If the Fed buys bonds from the nonbank public, the sellers will receive checks which they will most likely deposit as demand deposits in commercial banks. This constitutes a direct increase in the money supply plus an increase in the reserves of commercial banks which could lead to a further expansion in the money supply. If the Fed buys bonds directly from commercial banks, the banks' free reserves will be increased, thus increasing the potential for expanding the money supply.

In actuality, when the Fed buys bonds in the open market they usually come from both commercial banks and the nonbank public. The same is true for the sale of bonds. Therefore, in summary, when the Fed buys bonds it increases both the money supply and the potential for future expansion of the money supply by increasing the reserves of commercial banks. When it sells bonds, it decreases both the money supply and the potential for future expansion in the money supply by reducing the commercial banks' reserves.

When the Fed is deliberately increasing the money supply and the reserves of commercial banks, it is following an "easy-money policy." This means it is attempting to encourage increased lending and borrowing of money. The increased supply of loanable funds will probably result in lower interest rates as well as increased availability of credit. This should stimulate spending somewhat.

When the Fed is deliberately decreasing the money supply and the reserves of commercial banks, it is following a "tight-money policy." In this case, it is attempting to discourage lending and borrowing. Not only will credit be difficult to obtain, but also interest rates will be climbing. The purpose of a tight-money policy is to reduce total spending.

Changes in the Discount Rate

Federal Reserve Banks sometimes lend money at interest to their member commercial banks. The rate of interest which the Federal Reserve Banks charge commercial banks on such loans is called the discount rate.

Theoretically a commercial bank could borrow money from its Federal Reserve Bank at a discount rate of perhaps 5 percent and then relend the money to one of its customers at 7 percent, making a 2 percent profit on the loan. Suppose a commercial bank was following such a policy and the Fed raised the discount rate from 5 percent to 6 percent. How would the commercial bank react? If it wanted to maintain its customary profit of 2 percent it would probably raise the interest rate which it charged its customers from 7 percent to 8 percent. In other words, a rise in the discount rate would cause a rise in general interest rates.

In practice, commercial banks do not usually borrow large amounts from the Fed for purposes of relending. Most loans to commercial banks are of an emergency nature for purposes of replenishing reserves which have run dangerously low. Nevertheless, changes in the discount rate do tend to influence the interest rate which commercial banks charge their customers. Therefore, when the Fed increases the discount rate, a general tightening of credit and increase in interest rates tends to follow. Just the opposite is true of a reduction in the discount rate.

Moral Suasion

Moral suasion involves the use of oral and written appeals by the Fed in an attempt to exert pressure on bankers to expand or restrict credit. While it has been somewhat successful at times, it is usually far less effective than the other instruments discussed above. If a banker has funds which he can lend at interest, he is unlikely to forego this opportunity to increase his earnings just because the Fed desires a tightening of credit.

Margin Regulations

The Federal Reserve Board also has been given the authority by Congress to set the margin requirements on the purchases of stock. The margin requirement is the percentage downpayment which is required when borrowing to finance the purchase of stock. The excessive use of credit played a significant role in the stock market crash of 1929. Therefore, the Fed has been given the power to control credit buying of stock.

By increasing the margin requirement, the Fed is able to discourage speculation on borrowed funds. A decrease in margin requirements may stimulate activity in the stock market.

Using Monetary Policy Tools

While moral suasion and margin regulations are of some value to the monetary authorities, they are far less significant than the other three instruments discussed above. Open-market operations, changes in reserve requirements, and changes in the discount rate are powerful instruments which the Fed can use to regulate the banking system and bring about changes in the cost and availability of credit.

By far the most important and most frequently used of these three is open-market operations. Open-market operations can be used on a daily basis if necessary. They are the fine tuner of monetary policy in the sense that they can be used to bring about very small gradual changes in the money supply. On the other hand, they can also be used to bring about more drastic changes if necessary.

Changes in the reserve requirements can have a disruptive effect on the banking system and are therefore used only infrequently. However, this instrument can prove very useful at times if combined with open-market operations.

Changes in the discount rate are made rather frequently. In addition to the direct effect of a change in the discount rate, the public announcement that accompanies the change tends to inform the public of the general direction of monetary policy at that time.

The end purpose of all these monetary tools is to influence total spending and thus move aggregate demand closer to the level necessary for the maintenance of high employment with relatively stable prices. This end goal is accomplished by making changes in the availability and cost of credit. If the economy was suffering from excess aggregate demand which was causing demand-pull inflation, the Fed would pursue a tight-money policy. That is, it would make credit more difficult to obtain by reducing the reserves held by commercial banks, and also increase interest rates. This would tend to discourage borrowing and credit buying.

If the problem was one of substantial unemployment resulting from insufficient aggregate demand, the Fed would pursue an easy-money policy. Credit would be made more readily available by increasing the reserves of commercial banks, and interest rates would be lowered. This would hopefully tend to encourage increased borrowing and spending.

Monetary policy, by making changes in the cost and availability of credit, undoubtedly has some effect on all three components of aggregate demand (C + I + G). If credit is unavailable or interest rates are extremely high, consumers may be discouraged from making some purchases that they would otherwise make. Also, a local unit of government that is planning to sell bonds to finance a new building may decide to delay construction if the interest rate is extremely high.

However, the biggest impact of monetary policy is on the investment component of aggregate demand. A businessman will not borrow money for an investment project if the interest rate is higher than the expected return on the investment. Therefore, a tight-money policy with rising interest rates will have a tremendous impact on investment spending. If interest rates were driven high enough almost all investment spending would cease. Thus, a tight-money policy is extremely effective in curtailing investment spending.

Monetary policy is far more effective in curtailing investment spending than it is in stimulating investment. At times of insufficient aggregate demand the policy makers attempt to encourage increased spending. By pursuing an easy-money policy, the Fed can make credit more readily available and reduce interest rates. However, there is no certainty that businessmen will respond by increasing investment spending. You can lead a horse to water but you can't make him drink. Similarly, you can make investment funds available at low interest rates, but you cannot make businessmen borrow the funds and invest.

Usually during slack periods in the economy when aggregate demand is down, most businessmen find that they cannot sell all that they can produce. They may have to shut down part of their operation and operate below full capacity. Under such circumstances it is highly unlikely that businessmen will want to borrow money for expansion no matter how low the interest rate. During the depression of the 1930s, many businessmen would have refused to borrow for expansion purposes even at zero interest rate.

Thus, monetary policy is a powerful tool for curtailing investment spending during periods of excess demand. However, it is often ineffective as an instrument for stimulating investment spending in times of insufficient aggregate demand. Fiscal policy, which we shall examine next, is usually more effective than monetary policy for purposes of stimulating aggregate demand.

Summary

1. The Federal Reserve System consists of twelve separate Federal Reserve Banks under the central control of the Board of Governors. The Federal Reserve Banks are owned by the member banks in their district but their basic policies are established by the Board of Governors.

2. The Board of Governors is responsible for the general supervision and control of the money and banking system of the nation. Since the seven members of the Board of Governors are appointed by the President and confirmed by the Senate for fourteen-year staggered terms, monetary policy can be effectively separated from partisan politics.

3. The nation's money supply is officially defined as the total currency in circulation plus demand deposits. Demand deposits constitute nearly 80 percent of the money supply. The money supply is regulated by the Federal Reserve authorities. There is a relationship between the money supply and the price level, but the relationship is not a precise one.

4. Monetary policy influences the cost and availability of credit and thus the level of total spending. The instruments of monetary policy include changes in reserve

requirements, open-market operations, changes in the discount rate, moral suasion, and margin regulations.

5. Monetary policy is more effective in curtailing aggregate demand in times of inflation than it is in stimulating aggregate demand during times of recession and unemployment.

5 Fiscal Policy as a Means of Controlling Inflation & Unemployment

F iscal policy may be defined as the use of the government's taxing and spending powers in an effort to regulate economic activity in such a way as to achieve and maintain high employment with relatively stable prices. Fiscal policy tools include tax increases and decreases, and government spending increases and decreases.

The massive corporate and income tax cuts of 1964 represented a deliberate attempt to stimulate aggregate demand and reduce unemployment. The tax cuts of almost $11 billion came at a time when the federal budget was already incurring a deficit. In 1968 Congress enacted a 10 percent surtax in a deliberate attempt to curtail aggregate demand. Both of these tax changes are excellent examples of fiscal policy in action. A good example on the spending side involves the withholding of federal highway funds by the President in an effort to fight inflation. Also, every federal budget is formulated with the state of the economy in mind. If the economy is suffering from unemployment and insufficient aggregate demand, a planned deficit will probably be built into the budget. If the economy is suffering from inflation caused by excessive aggregate demand, a planned surplus may be built into the budget.

How Fiscal Policy Works

As we learned in the last chapter, monetary policy is used to influence the cost and availability of credit. Fiscal policy, on the other hand, is designed to influence the level of income directly. Both ultimately influence the level of total spending. While monetary policy makes its biggest impact on the investment component of aggregate demand, fiscal policy primarily affects consumption and government spending, although both have some effect on all three components of aggregate demand.

The total spending level (C + I + G) is affected by fiscal policy in the following ways. A tax increase will leave consumers with less take-home pay and thus reduce their spending. A tax cut will have just the opposite effect in that consumers will have more take-home pay and consequently will probably increase their spending. Increases and decreases in government spending will of course directly affect the government spending component of aggregate demand.

A change in the personal income tax directly affects the after-tax income of consumers. If the tax rate is increased, consumers will have less disposable income (income after taxes) than before. They could react to this situation in a variety of ways. For example, they could withdraw funds from savings to offset the loss in disposable income resulting from the tax increase. Also, they could borrow money to supplement the reduced disposable income. However, each of these potential solutions would be only a temporary answer for most individuals. Hence, for most consumers an increase in personal taxes and the resulting decrease in disposable income must inevitably lead to reduced spending. Therefore, if policy makers wish to decrease consumer spending, there is no surer way to accomplish this than to raise taxes and thus reduce disposable income.

Just the opposite is true of a tax reduction. A tax cut increases the disposable income of consumers. Consumers could react to a tax cut by putting the increased take-home pay in their savings accounts. However, most individuals will react to a tax cut by spending part or all of the increase in disposable income. Since most households operate on a very tight family budget, there is usually a substantial backlog of needs and wants which are just waiting for an additional source of income. If suddenly this week's take-home pay is three or four dollars higher than usual, the family will probably quickly find a "need" to spend the extra income on. Some families may add part of the increased disposable income to their savings but few families are likely to put it all in savings. Hence, tax increases and decreases generally prove effective in bringing about changes in consumer spending.

If a tax increase or decrease is also applied to the corporate income tax, investment spending may also be affected. Increases and decreases in the corporate income tax change the after-tax profits of corporations. A corporation may react to a tax cut by spending the additional after-tax profit for investment in new plant capacity. However, since investment decisions are based on many other factors such as the general business outlook, we cannot be sure that a corporate tax increase or decrease will affect investment spending.

On the spending side, policy makers are able to affect the incomes of individuals directly through changes in government spending. If the President withholds federal funds for such projects as interstate highways, he directly affects the employment and incomes of individuals involved in these projects. If a highway construction project is halted for lack of federal funds, construction workers will be dismissed. This will affect not only the incomes of these workers but also their spending plans, since an unemployed worker must usually severely restrict his spending. When the President releases the funds, just the opposite chain of events will occur.

Of far greater importance than the withholding and release of highway funds is the overall effect of the total federal budget. In recent years an important considera- tion in determining the size and structure of the federal budget has been the overall state of the economy. If the economy is suffering from substantial unemployment and a serious deficiency in aggregate demand, the budget will probably provide for a planned deficit. That is, the government will deliberately attempt to spend more than it will receive in the form of tax revenue.

The purpose of this deliberate deficit spending is to stimulate the economy and reduce unemployment. Since government spending is one of the three basic compo- nents of aggregate demand (C + I + G), increases in government spending will tend to increase aggregate demand unless it is offset by comparable decreases in consumer and/or investment spending. Since increased tax collections tend to decrease consumer spending, increases in government spending accompanied by increases in taxes may have little effect on the total spending level. In other words, the increases in govern- ment spending might be offset by similar decreases in consumer spending. Thus, deficit spending may be necessary at times in order to raise aggregate demand to the desired level.

If the economy is suffering from high inflation

resulting from excess aggregate demand, the proper medicine might be a surplus in the federal budget. The government may choose to spend less than it receives in the form of tax revenue. A reduction in government spending will tend to reduce aggregate demand unless offset by a comparable increase in consumer and/or investment spending.

In summary, fiscal policy works by increasing or decreasing the basic components of aggregate demand (C + I + G). Personal income tax changes tend to increase or decrease the level of consumer spending. Also, changes in corporate income taxes may have some effect on the level of investment spending, and government spending changes can have important direct effects on aggregate demand unless offset by changes in taxes. We will discuss various budget philosophies with regard to federal taxing and spending later in this chapter.

Discretionary and Nondiscretionary Fiscal Policy

Discussions on fiscal policy sometimes make a distinction between discretionary and nondiscretionary fiscal policy. Discretionary fiscal policy is the deliberate changing of taxes and government spending to offset cyclical fluctuations and maintain high employment with relatively stable prices. Nondiscretionary fiscal policy involves changes in tax receipts and government spending which occur automatically over the business cycle. Such changes arise from the kinds of taxes and expenditure programs which are built into our system and do not require deliberate action on the part of anyone.

Built-in Stabilizers

These automatic changes in tax collections and government expenditures are frequently referred to as "built-in stabilizers." In other words, they have a stabilizing effect on the economy. As a result of these built-in stabilizers, declines in the levels of aggregate demand and output tend automatically to create budget deficits, and increases in aggregate demand and output tend automatically to cause budget surpluses. The most important of the built-in stabilizers are the progressive federal income tax, and the unemployment compensation and welfare programs.

The Progressive Federal Income Tax.   We call the federal income tax a progressive tax. By this we mean that as one's income increases, his tax rate will also increase. In other words, the higher the income, the larger the percentage paid in taxes. Because the federal income tax has progressive rates, a rise in the national income will result in more than proportionate increases in government tax collections. As aggregate demand and output increase, more and more people will become employed and more overtime will be available to those already employed. As a result of this, government tax receipts will tend to increase automatically, thus putting the brakes on the economic expansion. Conversely, as aggregate demand and output decline, tax collections will fall more than proportionately, providing a cushioning effect. Hence, the progressive federal income tax tends automatically to cause increases and decreases in tax collections at the appropriate times. Unfortunately, these automatic changes are not of sufficient magnitude to accomplish the whole job of stabilizing the economy. They usually need to be supplemented with discretionary tax changes.

Unemployment Compensation and Welfare Programs.   During periods of recession when more and more workers become unemployed, there will be automatic increases in government spending in the form of unemployment compensation and relief payments. This will tend to cushion the recession. On the other hand, during periods of prosperity unemployment declines, thus reducing government spending for unemployment compensation. The number of people on relief should also decline. These automatic decreases in government spending tend to slow down the economic expansion and reduce inflationary pressures.

Unfortunately, none of the automatic or built-in stabilizers are sufficient to prevent recessions and booms. They work in the right direction and are beneficial, but they need to be supplemented by discretionary fiscal policy.

Problems of Executing Fiscal Policy

While fiscal policy could potentially be a very effective tool in managing the economy, it has some very troublesome limitations. It is therefore important that we examine some of the problems facing the policy makers in their use of fiscal policy.

Problems of Timing

It is very difficult to predict accurately when the economy is going to turn the corner from insufficient aggregate demand to excess demand and vice versa. Therefore, fiscal policy is usually put into effect only after inflation or recession is already a fact of life. This results in a time lag between the economic illness and the fiscal medicine. Many argue that this is like locking the barn door after the horse is gone. They argue that we should practice preventive medicine by using fiscal policy to head off inflation or unemployment before they begin. Unfortunately, economic forecasting is still too imperfect a science to permit this. The best that can be hoped for is to begin applying the brakes at the first sign of inflation and to hit the acceleration pedal as soon as recession becomes apparent. Even this procedure is not always possible. What do you do when inflation and recession occur simultaneously?

There is also the problem of lack of flexibility in

many spending programs. Many public works projects such as the building of dams and interstate highways require long planning and construction periods. A short period of insufficient aggregate demand and high unemployment may not be long enough for policy makers to implement or complete such projects.

Problems of Political Feasibility

Unfortunately, good economics and good politics are not always compatible. This fact poses one of the greatest of all obstacles to sound economic policy and probably constitutes the greatest source of weakness to fiscal policy.

To be effective, fiscal medicine must be administered as soon as possible after an economic illness has become evident. Yet, usually a period of many months will elapse between the time the President's economic advisers recommend fiscal policy measures and the time the measures are actually implemented, if indeed they are ever implemented. The tax cut enacted in February 1964 under the Johnson administration was first proposed by President Kennedy in early 1963. This kind of delay can sometimes be disastrous.

Suppose the economy is faced with a problem of excess demand and inflation, and the President's economic advisers decide that the best medicine would be a tax increase. How does the proposed tax increase get from the proposal stage to the implementation stage? First, the President must be convinced that it is the correct thing to do both economically and politically. Even if the President is convinced by his economic advisers that it is the proper medicine for the economy, he may be persuaded by his political advisers that it is bad politics to raise taxes, and the needed tax increase may not get beyond this point. This was partly the case with President Johnson in the mid-1960s. His economic advisers recommended a tax increase to offset the accelerating government spending in Vietnam and reduce the accompanying inflationary pressures. President Johnson was apparently persuaded that to ask the American people to pay higher taxes because of an increasingly unpopular war would not be good politics. Hence, he procrastinated in the hope that his economic advisers were wrong and the problem would go away. The problem did not go away and the 10 percent surcharge was finally introduced in Congress in 1968 some two to three years after it was initially needed.

Even if a President is above politics on such issues and recommends that Congress immediately enact the proposed tax increase, some members of Congress will certainly play politics with the issue. The proposed legislation may be held up in a congressional committee for months in order to avoid taking a stand on the controversial issue before election time. Even when it does come to a vote, it may be voted down for political rather than economic reasons. No congressman is likely to gain popularity in his district by voting for tax increases. Consequently, many congressmen who believe a tax increase is just what the economy needs may still feel they have to either vote against the measure or face defeat in the next election.

If the economy needs a tax cut instead of a tax increase, the situation is quite different. It is very unlikely that a President or congressman would ever be hurt politically by voting for a tax cut. On the contrary, a vote for lower taxes would almost certainly increase a politician's popularity. Unfortunately, there are times when the economy needs a tax increase as well as times when a tax cut is in order. However, many congressmen who are very willing to vote for a tax cut when the economy needs stimulation do not have the courage to vote for a tax increase when economic activity should be slowed down.

The overall effect of this political feasibility problem

is that needed fiscal policy measures may not be implemented at all, or may be implemented far too late to be effective. In fact, if the medicine is too late in coming the disease may have changed in the meantime. For example, if a proposed tax increase to halt inflation is too long in coming, the economy may have moved from an inflationary period to a period of recession and unemployment. Certainly a tax increase would not be the correct medicine for recession. It would only make the problem worse.

Problems of State and Local Finance

One additional complication of fiscal policy is that sometimes the effects of state and local finance at least partially offset the effects of federal fiscal policy. It would be desirable for government spending at all levels to move in the same direction from the viewpoint of economic stability. However, state and local governments often increase their spending during times of prosperity when the federal government is attempting to hold spending back in order to slow the economy down. Also, state and local governments sometimes reduce expenditures during times of recession. This is just the opposite of federal policy.

Budget Philosophies

Economists generally agree that unbalanced federal budgets are helpful in stabilizing the economy. At times of excess demand and inflation it is helpful for the government to spend less than the amount of its tax receipts, thus creating a surplus in the budget. At times of insufficient aggregate demand and high unemployment the government should spend more than it takes in, thus causing a deficit in the federal budget. This use of the federal budget as an instrument for managing the economy has caused considerable controversy and has led to the development of several budget philosophies. There are basically four budget philosophies: an annually balanced budget; a cyclically balanced budget; "functional finance"; and a high-employment balanced budget. Let us examine each of these budget philosophies.

Annually Balanced Budget

An annually balanced budget is one in which the government attempts to spend exactly the same amount that it takes in each year. While some political leaders and businessmen expound the virtues of an annually balanced budget, few economists would endorse such a policy.

In the first place, an annually balanced budget would be impossible to attain even if it were desirable. Neither government spending nor tax receipts are totally stable during any given year. While the proposed annual budget is usually a fixed amount, certain spending programs must be flexible by their very nature. For example, how much is to be spent on unemployment compensation during a given year? It depends on the amount of unemployment in the economy. If there is very little unemployment the expenditure for unemployment compensation will be small. But if the economy experiences a recession during the year, spending for this purpose may be substantial.

While the amount of spending cannot be absolutely predetermined at the beginning of the year, it is far more stable than the amount of tax collections. Tax receipts may be very unpredictable since they are determined by the level of employment and incomes. If we had a fixed head tax of so much per person we could simply multiply the amount by the number of persons and come up with an exact figure. However, the federal income tax is not so predictable. If I am unemployed and have no income during the year, I do not owe any tax. If I am fully employed at a high salary for the entire year, I owe a substantial tax. Since we cannot accurately predict the level of employment or income, we cannot accurately predict the amount of tax receipts which the government will receive in a given year. Consequently, an exactly balanced annual budget is not possible although an approximately balanced budget is a possibility.

Even if an annually balanced budget were feasible, it would be very undesirable from an economic viewpoint. Suppose the economy begins moving into a recession. The problem is one of insufficient aggregate demand, and the solution is an increase in one or more of the three basic components of aggregate demand (C + I + G). Since it is often difficult to stimulate investment during periods of recession, the most promising solution to the problem is to increase consumption and/or government spending. Are these actions compatible with maintaining a balanced budget? No, the goals of stimulating aggregate demand and balancing the budget are in conflict with one another.

When the economy begins slipping into a recession, tax collections begin to decline as more and more people become unemployed and have no income on which to pay taxes. The decline in tax receipts destroys the balance in the budget. If the government wishes to restore balance in the budget, it must either increase tax rates in order to collect more from those still employed, or it must reduce government spending to bring it in line with the reduced tax receipts.

Thus, the actions necessary to maintain approximate balance in the federal budget are just the opposite of those needed to fight recession and restore full employment. To balance the budget, we need to increase taxes and/or decrease government spending. To restore full employment we need to reduce taxes and/or increase government spending. We can't have it both ways. We must choose whether it is more important to maintain a balanced budget, or to use fiscal policy to promote high employment with relatively stable prices. For most economists the choice is easy. Wide fluctuations in the business cycle are far too high a price to pay for the maintenance of an annually balanced budget.

Cyclically Balanced Budget

A cyclically balanced budget is one which is balanced over the course of the business cycle. This means that there should be budget deficits during periods of recession and depression in order to stimulate the economy, and budget surpluses during periods of prosperity to curb inflation and help pay off the public debt incurred during the deficit years. In other words, there would be budget deficits in some years and budget surpluses in other years, and over a period of many years the two would roughly cancel each other.

Theoretically such a policy would permit the use of fiscal policy as a stabilizing instrument and at the same time preserve the long-term objective of budgetary balance. Unfortunately, business cycles do not fit a uniform pattern with equal periods of recession and prosperity. Consequently, it is extremely unlikely that the surpluses would just equal the deficits over any given period of years.

Functional Finance

Those who advocate functional finance as a budget philosophy argue that a balanced budget either annually or cyclically is of secondary importance. They believe that the government should use fiscal policy in any way necessary to achieve high employment with stable prices. If this results in a balanced budget over the long run, fine. But if it does not, they do not consider this a serious problem. Some conservative economists and political leaders are critical of this approach. They believe that there should be at least a long-term goal of balancing the budget as a precaution against runaway spending and inflation.

High-Employment Balanced Budget

The high-employment balanced budget is in a sense a compromise between those who advocate functional finance and those who advocate a cyclically balanced budget. Both President Kennedy and President Nixon supported this budget philosophy. Basically, this budget policy involves an attempt to formulate a budget that will be in balance or possibly even have a slight surplus if, and only if, the economy is operating at a high-employment level.

The policy makers select a high-employment level, such as 4 percent unemployment, which they regard as "full employment," and then compute the amount of tax revenue which would be forthcoming if the economy were operating at this level. They will then attempt to restrict spending to this level or slightly below it. Thus, if the economy were operating at this level of employment the amount of tax revenue would be equal to or slightly greater than the total spending. Hence, this would be a situation with a high-employment balanced budget, or possibly high-employment surplus.

President Nixon used this concept in referring to his budgets as having a "full-employment" surplus even though in actuality the budgets had large deficits. The reason the Nixon budgets showed such large deficits is that the unemployment rates were higher than administration officials expected. When unemployment increases, tax revenues decline. Consequently, a budget with a planned balance at the "full-employment" level will have a deficit when unemployment is high. This is good because a deficit in the federal budget tends to stimulate the economy and reduce unemployment.

A deficit simply means that the government is

pumping more money into the economy through government spending than it is pumping out in the form of tax collections. This additional spending power in the economy usually results in an increase in aggregate demand. As aggregate demand increases, total output and employment should also gradually increase. Therefore, so long as the economy is below the "full-employment" level, a budget deficit is desirable. As the economy moves closer and closer to the "full-employment" level, the deficit should get smaller and smaller until the budget finally becomes balanced or perhaps even has a slight surplus.

A high-employment balanced budget may not necessarily assure high employment. The automatic stimulation resulting from the built-in deficit may be insufficient to move the economy quickly toward "full employment." At times, it may be necessary to have more substantial and intentional deficits or surpluses than would automatically be provided. Nevertheless, it is probably superior to all the other budget philosophies.

The Public Debt

One cannot properly talk about fiscal policy and deficit spending without including some discussion of the public debt. The two are related. When there is a deficit in the federal budget the public debt goes up. In other words, when the federal government spends more than its income during a given year it borrows money by selling bonds to make up the difference. Many conservative politicians who oppose deficit spending do so because they fear an ever-increasing public debt.

Probably no other economic issue is surrounded by so much misunderstanding as the public debt. The man on the street generally views the debt with awe and sometimes outright fear. Editors write ominous editorials about it, and cartoonists sometimes depict the American people being crushed by this awesome menace. Yet, if a group of economists were to make a list of important economic problems the public debt would probably be near the bottom of the list if it were included at all. Since there is so much confusion over this issue, it is important that we examine the public debt in some detail.

Size and Source of Debt

The public debt today is close to half a trillion dollars. This is an astronomical figure which almost defies comprehension. How did we ever incur such a large debt and how fast is it growing? The answer to the first question is that the primary source of the debt is World War II and the cold wars, and not deficits incurred as a result of countercyclical fiscal policy. As a result of World War II, the public debt grew from $50.9 billion in 1940 to $259.5 billion in 1946. This constitutes more than a fivefold increase in a six-year period.

While the absolute amount of the debt has grown consistently since World War II, it has not grown nearly as rapidly as the wealth and productive capacity of the economy. In fact, the public debt as a percent of the gross national product has consistently declined since 1946. Obviously a wealthy nation is better able to carry a large debt than a poor nation. Thus, if a nation's wealth and income grow more rapidly than its debt, it is unrealistic to assert that the debt burden is getting greater.

The Differences Between Public and Private Debt

The greatest source of confusion over the public debt is probably the failure to recognize the basic differences between a public and a private debt. If I as an individual owe a debt to another individual, I am poorer because of it. Such is not the case with the public debt. Absurd as it may sound, the people of the United States owe the public debt to the people of the United States. In other words, we owe the debt to ourselves. If I borrow money from one of my pockets to put in the other pocket, I am neither richer nor poorer. Similarly, the United States is neither richer nor poorer because of the public debt.

Probably a source of confusion for some people is the erroneous belief that the public debt (sometimes referred to as the national debt) is owed to foreign nations. Such is not the case. We do not owe the debt to England, France, Russia, or any other foreign nation. If we did, it would be an international debt and would be comparable to a private debt with all its burdens.

We the taxpayers of the United States owe the public debt to the holders of U.S. government securities who, with some insignificant exceptions, happen to be citizens of the United States. If we were to decide to pay off the public debt, some of us who own no government securities would be poorer due to the higher taxes. But others of us who own government securities would be richer. However, the nation would be neither richer nor poorer as a result of paying off the national debt. Of course, the public debt will never have to be paid off. It is continually refinanced by selling new bonds in order to get funds to pay off those bonds which are maturing. In other words, those persons to whom we owe the debt change from time to time.

Some False Fears About the Debt

While the public debt does cause some real burdens, the fears about the debt which most people hold are unjustified. Let us examine some of these false fears.

The Debt May Lead to National Bankruptcy. This fear is the result of the failure to understand the differences between a private and public debt. If an individual gets too deeply into debt, he may become unable to pay his debts and eventually go bankrupt. This could not happen to the United States. In the first place, there is no need for the debt ever to be paid off. As government bonds mature new bonds can be sold to the same or new investors, and the debt can be continually refinanced. At this point I am sure that many readers will immediately ask the following question. What if people lose confidence in the government and refuse to buy government securities? This question can be answered by another question. Where can investors find a more secure investment than in U.S. government securities? If the government were to fall, all private investments would also probably become worthless. It would be possible for some of our largest and soundest corporations to go bankrupt without the government falling. However, it is highly unlikely that our government could fall without affecting private investments. Hence, government securities probably provide the safest investment opportunities available. By raising the interest yield on government securities sufficiently high, the government can probably always attract sufficient funds to refinance and/or expand the public debt.

Of course, continuous refinancing of the debt is only one way for the nation to avoid bankruptcy. Suppose the government could not borrow sufficient money to pay off old debts. The government could always raise taxes or even print new money to pay off the debt. While these would be undesirable actions, the government would have the legal right to take such actions if it believed they were necessary. Thus, there is no way in which the public debt could lead to national bankruptcy.

Interest Payments Will Impoverish the Nation.   This fear also involves the failure to differentiate between a private and public debt. An individual who is deeply in debt finds that a substantial portion of his income is required just to pay the interest on the debt. A comparable situation would be an international debt. If we owed the public debt to Russia or

England instead of to the American people, interest payments on the debt would constitute a real burden on the nation. Such an international debt would cause a constant drain on the nation's resources and the nation would be poorer each time it made an interest payment. However, we do not owe the debt to foreign nations. We owe it to those Americans who have chosen to invest in government securities. Since all taxpayers must contribute to the interest payments and only some Americans own government securities, interest payments involve transfer payments from all Americans to some Americans. However, the nation is neither richer nor poorer because of the interest payments.

The Debt Will Burden Future Generations. Frequently one will hear the public debt denounced on the grounds that through our extravagance today we are imposing heavy burdens on our children and grandchildren. Such is not the case with the public debt. In many other respects, such as extravagant use of some natural resources, and pollution of the environment, we are probably creating hardships for future generations. However, the public debt will not prove to be any more of a burden on our children or grandchildren than it is on the present generation. As we have said, the public debt will never have to be paid off. Hence, our grandchildren will not have to pay off a debt for which we are responsible. However, suppose our grandchildren were to decide to pay off the debt. To whom will they pay the debt? The answer is simple. If our grandchildren decide to pay off the public debt, they will make payment to our grandchildren. The same is true of interest payments. When future generations make interest payments, these payments will be made to those members of that generation who have chosen to put their money in government securities.

As we have seen, a large proportion of the public

debt was incurred during World War II. Does this mean that the war generation borrowed from future generations in order to finance the war? No, the war was primarily paid for by those who were living at that time. The American people of that generation had to make great sacrifices in order to provide resources for the war. Automobile production was terminated and many other consumer items were unavailable. The war generation paid for the war in spite of the fact that a large debt was accumulated during this period. The war could perhaps have been financed entirely out of taxes, but such action would have imposed tremendous hardships on many people. Instead, the government chose to borrow substantial funds from those who were willing and able to invest in government securities.

To the extent that war expenditures prevented the construction of new factories and other capital goods for future production, a burden was placed on future generations. However, this burden was caused by the war and not by the public debt. The same burden would have existed if the war had been financed entirely by taxes.

Some Real Burdens of the Debt

While the existence of a large public debt is not nearly as serious as most people believe, there are some real negative effects. One problem involves the probable redistribution of income that takes place when interest on the debt is paid. Most government bondholders tend to be in the middle and upper-income brackets. Since all taxpayers have to contribute to the interest payments, and only those who own bonds receive any of the payments, it is likely that interest payments on the public debt contribute to greater income inequality. However, since these interest payments constitute a very small percentage of the national income, the redistribution effects are probably of minor significance.

A second real burden of the public debt is that it tends to contribute to inflation at times. Government securities are highly liquid and can easily be converted into cash. It is frequently argued that government bonds provide a potential backlog of purchasing power which can contribute to inflation in times of full employment.

A third possible real burden of the public debt is that the government is more likely to engage in wasteful spending if deficit financing is readily available. It is frequently argued that politicians would be more cautious in their spending if all spending had to be financed directly through taxation.

A Positive Aspect of the Debt

We learned in Chapter 4 that open-market operations constitute the most important monetary policy instrument available to the Federal Reserve Authorities. Yet, the buying and selling of government securities in the open market would not be possible without the existence of a large public debt. For this reason, some economists consider the public debt more of an advantage than a burden.

Summary

1. Fiscal policy involves the use of the government's taxing and spending powers in an effort to regulate aggregate demand in such a way as to achieve and maintain high employment without inflation. Discretionary fiscal policy is the deliberate changing of taxes and government spending to offset cyclical fluctuations. Nondiscretionary fiscal policy involves changes in tax receipts and government spending which occur automatically over the business cycle because of "built-in stabilizers."

2. Tax increases and decreases affect the disposable income of consumers and thus influence the level of

consumption spending. Increases and decreases in government spending will directly affect aggregate demand unless offset by changes in consumption and/or investment spending.

3. Problems faced by the policy makers in executing fiscal policy include time lags between economic illness and fiscal medicine, political obstacles, and offsetting effects of state and local finance.

4. Unbalanced federal budgets are helpful in stabilizing the economy. A budget surplus is helpful at times of excess demand and inflation. At times of insufficient aggregate demand and high unemployment a budget deficit is in order.

5. There are basically four budget philosophies: an annually balanced budget; a cyclically balanced budget; "functional finance," and a high-employment balanced budget.

6. The public debt engenders much misunderstanding and controversy. While the absolute amount of the public debt has grown consistently since World War II, the public debt as a percent of the GNP has consistently declined since 1946. Although the public debt does cause some real burdens, many of the fears about the debt are unjustified.

6 A Coordination of Monetary & Fiscal Policies

In the previous two chapters we examined the various monetary-policy and fiscal-policy tools available for regulating the economy. In this chapter we shall consider the need for coordination of monetary and fiscal policies, and the importance of different policy combinations for different economic ailments. As a first step, let us review the various policy actions which can be taken to regulate the economy.

Policy Possibilities:
An Examination of the Arsenal

As we have seen, the policy makers have a substantial arsenal of monetary and fiscal-policy weapons which can be used to fight inflation and unemployment. This kit of economic instruments is summarized in Table 4. Let us briefly examine the operation of each of these policy actions.

Actions to Curtail Aggregate Demand and Reduce Inflationary Pressures

The following monetary and fiscal policy actions are designed to curtail spending and reduce inflationary pressures. While some are more effective than others, they all tend to work in the right direction.

Selling Government Securities in the Open Market. When the Federal Reserve Authorities sell government securities in the open market they pump money out of the economy. Payments for government securities sold usually come both from commercial banks and the non-bank public. Hence, the money supply is directly decreased, and there is a decrease in the reserves and thus the lending capacity of commercial banks. Consequently, there is a decrease in the availability of credit. There may also be an accompanying increase in interest rates as a result of the decreased supply of potential credit.

How does this decreased availability, and possible increase in cost, of credit affect aggregate demand? Primarily, through decreases in investment spending. As credit becomes more difficult to obtain and more costly, businessmen will be forced to curtail their investment expenditures. Thus, open-market operations as well as the other monetary-policy instruments have their biggest impact on the investment component of aggregate demand, although consumption and local government spending may be somewhat affected.

Raising the Discount Rate.   As we learned in Chapter 4, the discount rate is the rate of interest which commercial banks must pay on funds borrowed from

Table 4

Policy Possibilities for Regulating Economic Activity

Actions Which Will Tend to Curtail Aggregate Demand and Reduce Inflationary Pressures:

Monetary-Policy Actions
1. Selling government securities in the open market.
2. Raising the discount rate.
3. Raising reserve requirements.

Fiscal-Policy Actions
1. Decreasing government spending.
2. Increasing taxes.

Actions Which Will Tend to Stimulate Aggregate Demand and Reduce Unemployment:

Monetary-Policy Actions
1. Buying government securities in the open market.
2. Lowering the discount rate.
3. Lowering reserve requirements.

Fiscal-Policy Actions
1. Increasing government spending.
2. Reducing taxes.

their Federal Reserve Bank. If the discount rate which commercial banks must pay increases, they will usually raise the interest rates which they charge their customers. Consequently, an increase in the discount rate will usually signal a general increase in interest rates. The increased cost of credit resulting from the rise in the discount rate will tend to discourage borrowing and spending, thus reducing aggregate demand and inflationary pressures.

Raising Reserve Requirements.   When the Federal Reserve Authorities increase the percentage of deposits which commercial banks must hold as reserves, they reduce the lending capacity of banks. This will result in a reduced availability of credit and probably higher interest rates, thus discouraging borrowing and spending. While this instrument of monetary policy is infrequently used, it can be an effective tool at times.

Decreasing Government Spending.   Most policy instruments have only an indirect effect on aggregate demand. However, since government spending is one of the three basic components of aggregate demand, any government spending change directly affects the level of total spending. Decreases in government spending directly reduce aggregate demand unless offset by increases in investment and/or consumption spending. Thus, reductions in government spending may be more effective in bringing about a rapid reduction in total spending and inflationary pressures than some of the other policy instruments. However, reductions in government spending may have some undesirable side effects. For example, a reduction in spending for highway construction and improvement may result in an increase in the death rate on the nation's highways.

Increasing Taxes.   An increase in taxes will tend to reduce aggregate demand because disposable income will be reduced. An increase in personal income taxes will leave consumers with less take-home pay. At first, consumers may attempt to offset this loss in disposable income by increased borrowing or withdrawals from savings. However, eventually the reduction in disposable income must result in reduced consumption spending.

An increase in corporate income taxes may result in a reduction in investment spending. Since corporations will have less after-tax profits, they will be forced to curtail investment spending, reduce dividend payments, or finance an increased proportion of investment projects with borrowed funds.

*Actions to Stimulate Aggregate Demand
and Reduce Unemployment*

The following policy actions are just the opposite of those listed in the above section. They are designed to increase rather than decrease aggregate demand.

Buying Government Securities in the Open Market. The purchase of government securities in the open market by the Federal Reserve Authorities usually involves payments both to commercial banks and to nonbank sellers of securities. Hence, money is pumped into the economy. The money supply is directly increased, and the reserves and lending capacity of commercial banks are also increased. Consequently, credit will become more readily available, and interest rates probably will decline. It is to be hoped that the end result of this chain of events will be an increase in investment spending and possibly some increase in the spending of consumers. Such an increase in aggregate demand would cause employers to increase their output and employment.

Lowering the Discount Rate. As we have already learned, a change in the discount rate usually signals a similar change in interest rates in general. Thus, a lowering of the discount rate will tend to reduce the cost of borrowing and hopefully increase the level of total spending. Again, an increase in aggregate demand will tend to reduce unemployment.

Lowering Reserve Requirements. A reduction in the percentage of total deposits which commercial banks are required to hold as reserves will increase their lending potential. Such action will tend to make credit more readily available, probably at lower interest rates. This should hopefully stimulate some increase in investment spending.

Increasing Government Spending. Just as decreases in government spending have a direct downward impact on aggregate demand, increases in government spending provide a sure method of increasing aggregate demand. Consequently, there is probably no other policy action which can have a more rapid direct impact on employment than an increase in government spending. This is true whether the increased government spending goes for a public works project or the purchase of additional armaments. In either case, additional workers will be required and unemployment will be reduced.

Reducing Taxes. A reduction in personal income taxes means an increase in disposable income for consumers. Although consumers could save the entire increase in take-home pay, this is not usually the case. Usually consumers will react to a tax cut by spending a large proportion of the additional disposable income. Therefore, a tax cut also provides a rather certain method of increasing aggregate demand and reducing un-employment.

A reduction in corporate income taxes may also increase investment. Since corporations will have larger after-tax profits, they may choose to use some of the additional funds for investment purposes.

The Proper Policy at the Right Time

Economists are often asked: Which works best, monetary policy or fiscal policy? There is no simple answer to this question. Monetary and fiscal policy both have their own strengths and weaknesses. Which one will be most effective in a certain situation depends on a variety of factors. Usually some combination of the two is best. Let us examine some of the strengths and weaknesses of each.

Advantages of Monetary Policy

Monetary policy has certain advantages relative to fiscal policy. Some of these advantages are listed below.

Can Be Implemented Rapidly. One of the biggest advantages of monetary policy is the speed with which decisions can be made and implemented. The decision-making power for monetary policy lies in the hands of the Board of Governors of the Federal Reserve System. They can act without consulting the President or Congress. If the Board believes the economy needs a tight-money policy, they can begin implementing such a policy immediately by using the various policy instruments available to them. Contrast this with the probable congressional delay of months before enacting a needed tax increase.

Usually Effective in Curtailing Demand. A tight-money policy, if pursued long enough and intensely enough, can almost certainly be effective in curtailing aggregate demand and reducing demand-pull inflationary pressures. Unfortunately, monetary policy is less effective in combating administered-price inflation and unemployment. However, if the problem of the economy is primarily one of excess aggregate demand and demand-pull inflation, monetary policy can be a very powerful and effective weapon.

Nonpolitical. Since the seven members of the Board of Governors are appointed for fourteen-year terms and are ineligible for reappointment, they are effectively insulated from partisan politics. Hence, their decisions can be based on economic rather than political considerations. Unfortunately, this is often not the case with fiscal policy.

Nondiscriminatory. Monetary policy is nondiscriminatory in the sense that actions taken by the Board of Governors are designed to apply to the economy as a whole and not to any particular group or groups. In the case of fiscal policy, decisions have to be made which will usually affect some groups more than others. For example, if the government increases spending, to whom or for what are they going to increase spending? Also, a proposed tax increase or decrease may be designed to affect high-income taxpayers differently than low-income taxpayers.

Although monetary policy is not deliberately discriminatory, it can be argued that some groups and industries are more adversely affected by a tight-money policy than others. For example, the housing industry is severely affected by a tight-money policy. Potential homeowners, who are either unable to obtain mortgage loan money or unwilling to pay the high interest rates, frequently defer their building plans until the tight-money period has ended. Consequently, building contractors are seriously injured by a tight-money policy.

Disadvantages of Monetary Policy

The advantages of monetary policy are partially offset by an equally long list of disadvantages. The most important disadvantages are listed below.

May Be Ineffective in Stimulating Demand. Although monetary policy can be very effective in curtailing excessive aggregate demand, it is far less potent as an instrument for stimulating aggregate demand and reducing unemployment. If the economy is suffering from insufficient aggregate demand and rising unemployment, monetary policy may be of little value as a remedy. The monetary authorities can make credit readily available at low interest rates, but they cannot compel businessmen to borrow the funds and invest them. If the general business outlook is dim, businessmen may be unwilling to borrow for purposes of expanding their capacity no matter how low the interest rate.

When it comes to stimulating aggregate demand, monetary policy is more of a carrot than a stick. An analogy can be made between monetary policy and driving a stubborn horse. By pulling tightly on the reins, the driver can slow the horse down or stop him. Similarly, a tight-money policy can hold the economy back and prevent runaway inflation. However, the driver of the horse will find that by loosening the reins he cannot necessarily make the horse go. The loose reins give the horse the opportunity to go if he chooses to, but if he is stubborn he may need to be prodded with a stick. Similarly, an easy-money policy provides the opportunity for aggregate demand to increase but does not force it to do so. Often the economy needs to be prodded also. Generally, fiscal policy is a far more effective prod than monetary policy.

Ineffective in Controlling Administered-Price Inflation. In Chapter 2 we examined administered-price inflation and saw that it can exist when there is no general excess demand. Unfortunately, monetary policy is ineffective in combating this type of inflation. To the extent that administered-price inflation exists simultaneously with substantial unemployment, a tight-money policy would probably increase unemployment more than it would reduce inflation.

Weakened by Financial Intermediaries. Financial intermediaries such as savings and loan associations, insurance companies, personal finance companies, and credit unions constitute a very large and important source of nonbank credit in this nation. Since these institutions are not commercial banks, they are not under the control of the Federal Reserve System. Consequently, restrictive monetary policies by the Federal Reserve System may be partially offset by the lending operations of these financial intermediaries.

Conflicts With Treasury Objectives. Since the United States Treasury is almost continually selling new bonds to refinance the public debt, it is interested in maintaining low interest rates. A difference of 1 percent in the interest rate on government securities may cost the government several billion dollars. However, during times of excess aggregate demand the monetary authorities are interested in maintaining high interest rates in an effort to curtail demand. Hence, there is often a basic conflict between the objectives of the Federal Reserve Authorities and those of the U.S. Treasury.

Forecasting Problems and Effect Lag.   Although monetary policy decisions can be rapidly made and implemented, it takes time for them to have their impact on the economy. It may take several months for a change in monetary policy to affect spending. Since monetary policy does not take immediate effect, it is important to be able to forecast accurately the state of the economy months in advance in order to initiate the proper monetary policy today. Unfortunately, economic forecasting is far from being an exact science. It is possible that by the time a tight-money policy begins to show up in decreased spending the economy may have turned the corner toward recession. In such a case the tight-money policy might prove to be more of a poison than a medicine.

Advantages of Fiscal Policy

Fiscal policy also has certain advantages and disadvantages relative to monetary policy. Two of the most important advantages are listed below.

Directly Affects Aggregate Demand.   While monetary policy affects spending only indirectly through changes in the availability and cost of credit, changes in government spending have a direct effect on aggregate demand. Also, tax changes, once they are initiated, tend to bring faster results than monetary policy. The problem of fiscal policy is the delay in initiating the action. Once the action is initiated, results tend to come much faster than they do from monetary policy.

Effective in Both Directions.   While monetary

policy is far more effective in curtailing excess demand and inflationary pressures than it is in stimulating demand during recession, fiscal policy tends to work in both directions. During times of demand-pull inflation, higher taxes and reduced government spending can be very helpful in curtailing aggregate demand. Similarly, lower taxes and increased government spending can help to move the economy out of a recession by increasing aggregate demand and thus reducing unemployment. This ability to combat recession and unemployment probably constitutes the biggest advantage of fiscal policy over monetary policy.

Disadvantages of Fiscal Policy

Like monetary policy, fiscal policy also has certain disadvantages and limitations. Let us examine some of the more important limitations.

Political Obstacles.   Probably the most important limitations to fiscal policy are political in nature. Good economics and good politics are often in conflict. Higher taxes might be good for the economy, but voting for increased taxes might be political suicide for some congressmen. Consequently, it may take months to get a needed tax increase through Congress. By the time the tax increase takes effect, economic conditions may have changed to the point that a tax cut rather than a tax increase is the proper medicine.

The same problem exists with spending changes. A congressman may be reluctant to vote for a needed increase in government spending unless some of the increased spending will filter into his district. Similarly, congressmen may oppose reductions in government spending if the reductions will adversely affect projects in their home districts.

Thus, although fiscal policy can have a rather direct and immediate impact on the economy once it is implemented, political considerations often cause long delays in the implementation of such policies. These delays can sometimes have disastrous effects on the economy.

Lack of Flexibility.   In addition to the political obstacles to flexible fiscal policy, there is also the problem of having desirable projects ready for funding at the time there is a need for increased government spending. It is easy to say that in times of recession the government should increase its spending. But what is the government going to spend the increased money on? Certainly there are always needs for more highways, dams, and so forth. However, these projects take long planning periods before actual construction can start. By the time they get to the construction stage, the economy may no longer need an increase in spending.

Conflicts With Other Objectives.   Using fluctuations in government spending as a countercyclical policy instrument poses a very serious problem. When it comes time to cut government spending in order to fight inflation, which items in the budget are to be cut? Which programs and employees are to be terminated? Such questions are not easily answered since any cut is going to affect someone adversely.

Certainly there should never be a deliberately wasteful increase in government spending just for the sake of stimulating the economy. Any increases in spending should be for projects that can be justified on their own merits. Hence, if a project is worthwhile and needed this year during a period of recession, is it any less worthwhile next year when the economy is suffering from excess demand? This problem has led some experts to favor tax changes as the primary fiscal policy instrument, thus avoiding deliberate changes in government spending.

The Proper Policy Mix

We have seen that neither monetary nor fiscal policy

is a panacea for all economic ills. Furthermore, there is no combination of the two which will solve all our economic problems. Nevertheless, some combination of monetary and fiscal policy is usually considered a more effective remedy for most economic ailments than a straight dose of one or the other.

Determining the proper mix of monetary and fiscal policy for the economy at any given time is a formidable task. However, there are certain guidelines which are helpful in determining the proper policy. Let us examine four possible combinations of monetary and fiscal policy.

Easy-Money—Easy-Fiscal Policy

A combination of easy-money and easy-fiscal policies would be in order during periods of severe recession or depression with little or no problem of inflation. The basic problem during such times is a deficiency of aggregate demand. Consequently, any actions to stimulate any or all of the three basic components of aggregate demand would be in order. Making credit more readily available at lower interest rates would at least provide the opportunity for increased credit spending. An increase in government spending would directly increase aggregate demand, and a reduction in taxes would give consumers a larger disposable income from which to spend.

Tight-Money—Tight-Fiscal Policy

Both a tight-money policy and a tight-fiscal policy would be appropriate if the economy were operating at full employment with substantial excess demand and very strong inflationary pressures. The objective would be to reduce aggregate demand to the proper level to eliminate the inflationary pressures without creating substantial unemployment. A tight-money policy with a reduced availability of credit and higher interest rates would tend to curtail investment spending. A reduction in government spending and an increase in taxes would reduce the other two components of aggregate demand.

While the above prescription could theoretically be appropriate under certain conditions, in most cases it would probably constitute too strong a dose of medicine. If aggregate demand is curtailed too much, we simply trade a problem of serious inflation for a problem of serious unemployment. Hence, if a combination of both tight-money and tight-fiscal policy is used, it is important that neither be extremely tight.

Easy-Money—Tight-Fiscal Policy

One of the problems of using a tight-money policy to combat inflation is that its primary impact is on investment, and a reduction in investment usually means a reduction in economic growth. By economic growth, we mean increases in the nation's capacity to produce goods and services. Investment spending goes for such things as new factories and new machines, and a curtailment of investment means less productive capacity in the future.

One potential solution to this problem is to use a tight-fiscal policy to control inflation, and pursue an easy-money policy to encourage continued investment. Such a policy puts the burden of curtailing inflation on the consumption and government spending components of aggregate demand rather than on investment. Increased taxes force consumers to spend less, thus freeing resources for increased investment which will in the long run result in increased supplies of goods and services. While such a policy probably has some merit, it is not likely to be very popular with consumers.

Tight-Money—Easy-Fiscal Policy

A combination of a tight-money and an easy-fiscal policy has sometimes been advocated as a solution to the conflict between full employment and our international balance of payments. The international balance of payments is an expression which refers to the relationship between the total flow of money out of the country and the total inflow of money into the country. When we buy goods from abroad, there is an outflow of money. When we sell goods, there is an inflow. However, imports and exports are only one source of the international money flow. Another important source is the flow of investment funds from one nation to another. It is important that the total flow of money out of a nation does not exceed the total inflow. If it does, there is a deficit in the balance of payments. Unfortunately, the United States has experienced serious deficits in its balance of payments in recent years.

One proposed solution to the problem is a tight-money policy which would tend to reduce inflationary pressures and lower prices, thus making our goods more competitive in world markets. A tight-money policy would also raise interest rates in the United States relative to those of other nations, thus discouraging the flow of investment funds out of the country and encouraging an inflow of investment funds. Such a tight-money policy, however, would tend to curtail aggregate demand and create unemployment unless offset by an easy fiscal policy.

Although such a combination might achieve the objectives of improving the balance of payments position and avoiding high unemployment, it would be costly in terms of economic growth. You will note that it is just the opposite of the prescription given above for encouraging investment and economic growth.

Summary

1. The policy makers have a substantial arsenal of weapons which can be used to fight inflation and unemployment. Actions to curtail aggregate demand and

fight inflation include: selling government securities in the open market; raising the discount rate; raising reserve requirements; decreasing government spending; and increasing taxes. Actions to stimulate aggregate demand and reduce unemployment include: buying government securities in the open market; lowering the discount rate; lowering reserve requirements; increasing government spending; and reducing taxes.

2. The advantages of monetary policy as a means of regulating the economy include: rapid implementation, effectiveness in curtailing aggregate demand, and the fact that it is nonpolitical and nondiscriminatory. The disadvantages include: ineffectiveness in stimulating aggregate demand and controlling administered-price inflation, weakening effect of financial intermediaries, conflicts with Treasury objectives, and effect lags.

3. An important advantage of fiscal policy as an instrument of economic control is the fact that it is effective both in increasing and in decreasing aggregate demand. Disadvantages of fiscal policy include: political obstacles, lack of flexibility, and conflicts with other objectives.

4. A combination of monetary and fiscal policy is usually considered a more effective remedy for most economic ailments than a straight dose of one or the other. Determining the proper mix of monetary and fiscal policy for the economy at any given time is a formidable task. However, there are certain guidelines which are helpful in determining the proper policy mix.

7 Other Methods of Controlling Inflation & Unemployment

Although monetary and fiscal policy tools have been the mainstay of government economic policy in recent years, they are not the only means of economic control. As we have seen, monetary and fiscal policy tools are insufficient to maintain high employment with stable prices at certain times. Therefore, it is important that we examine other potential methods of economic control.

Other Methods of Controlling Inflation

Other methods of controlling inflation usually involve some type of artificial market controls, such as the recent wage-price controls under the Nixon administration. However, they can also involve long-term programs for increasing supplies of vital items such as food and fuels. We shall examine both approaches in this chapter. Let us begin by looking at wage-price controls.

Wage-Price Controls

There has been much debate recently over the value of wage-price controls in controlling inflation. Those who argue that wage-price controls do not work point to the recent controls under the Nixon administration as proof. They emphasize the fact that we are now experiencing some of the worst inflation in recent history, and often argue that the high inflation following the controls was partly caused by the controls.

This outright denunciation of any controls on any wages or prices because the recent controls did not prove totally effective is somewhat unfair. The Nixon approach to wage-price controls is only one of many possible approaches, and many economists who advocate some form of partial controls would join those who denounce the recent controls. The next chapter is devoted to the special problems of the 1970s, and we will examine the wage-price controls of the Nixon administration in some detail. However, our purpose here is to examine the various possible approaches to wage-price controls in a more general sense.

Total Wage and Price Freezes.   A total wage and price freeze on the economy simply means that it is unlawful for any wage or price to increase. Such an action can be justified only on an emergency basis, and then for only a very short period of time. The ninety-day freeze announced in August 1971 was intended primarily to hold the line while the administration attempted to set up a more permanent and flexible mechanism of control. Unfortunately, the mechanism which was set up did not prove effective for a variety of reasons, which we shall examine in the next chapter.

There are several reasons why a permanent freeze on all wages and prices would be disastrous for the economy. Let us begin with some of the more obvious problems with which the reader should already be familiar. First of all, there is a problem of equity. No matter when a freeze is announced, there will always be some individuals who have just received a wage increase and others who are just about to receive an increase. Is it fair to deny a wage increase to individuals simply because it was scheduled to come one day, one week, or one month after the freeze, when those individuals who got a wage increase just a day or so before the freeze are unaffected?

Similarly, some businessmen will have just announced a price increase while others will have imminent price increases scheduled. Since a wage-price freeze must be announced without advance warning to be effective, many individuals and businesses will be penalized simply because their scheduled wage or price increases were one or two days too late.

A second problem is one of enforcement. In an economy as large and complex as ours it is absolutely impossible to prevent widespread violations of the freeze. Goods which are in short supply will be sold illegally at prices above the legal limit. Thus, not only will prices not be stabilized, but the attempt to do so will also contribute to increased crime.

The problems listed above are dwarfed by the one we are about to discuss. A permanent freeze on all wages and prices would literally destroy our economic system and lead to shortages undreamed of before. Fluctuating prices are the primary means of avoiding substantial shortages and surpluses in our economy. Without them our market system cannot function.

When a shortage of a particular item begins to develop, prices rise. This is because of the fact that the demand for the item is greater than the supply at current prices, and only through higher prices will the supply and demand be equated. In other words, as the price rises some individuals, who would have bought the item at the old price, are unwilling to pay the higher price. Thus, those individuals who are willing to pay the higher price will be the ones to get the scarce item.

Rationing out the reduced supply of the item is only one of the functions of the higher price. It also serves to encourage greater production of the scarce item. Often a product becomes scarce because it is no longer profitable to produce it at the current market price. However, the shortage results in higher prices which make the product more profitable to produce, and may ultimately result in an increased supply and possibly even lower prices again.

Agricultural products provide an excellent example of the above situation. If a freeze is placed on the price of beef at a price too low to make production profitable, beef producers will gradually go out of business and ultimately there will be no beef available. However, in the absence of a freeze, the market system will tend to solve the problem. If beef prices are too low to make production profitable, producers will begin curtailing production. As production is cut back a shortage of beef will arise, and consumers will begin pushing prices up by competing for the short supply of beef. As prices of beef rise, producers will find production again profitable and will begin expanding production. As beef production is expanded and the supply increases, prices will again begin to fall.

Hence, fluctuating prices serve a very important purpose in preventing overproduction or underproduction of the various goods and services in our economy. In a dynamic complex economy such as ours, the quantities of various goods and services demanded fluctuate from time to time. For example, consumers may decide they want more beef and less pork, or more bicycles and fewer automobiles. How do they signal these changed desires to producers? They do so by voting in the market place with their dollars. If a particular good receives an increased number of dollar votes, there will be a temporary shortage and prices will rise. The rise in price will signal the producers to increase production. If, for example, the price of beef rises substantially relative to that of pork, many pork producers will switch to beef production and the consumers will get the additional beef they desire.

Thus, it would be unthinkable to impose a permanent wage-price freeze on our economy. However, this does not mean that no artificial controls of any kind should ever be placed on the economy.

Partial Controls. A frequently ignored fact is that we have had price controls on parts of the economy for years. Public utility companies do not have the freedom to raise their rates without government permission. Public utilities have monopoly power in the areas in which they operate. That is, there is only one electric company or one telephone company in any given area. If you do not like the service which your telephone company provides, or if you believe the rates are too high, you cannot switch to a different company. You must continue with your present company or do without service. This monopoly power has been granted by the government because competition would not be practical in the case of public utilities. It would obviously be wasteful and senseless to have two or three sets of competing electric lines, or telephone lines, running down each rural road or city street. Consequently, there is only one public utility company in each area.

Suppose your telephone company or electric company were allowed to set whatever rate they believed justified. Would your utility bills increase? It is likely that they would increase substantially. Every individual and every business has a natural urge to increase their income when possible, and seldom will an individual or company admit to excessive earnings. Thus, some form of control is necessary to prevent exploitation.

The usual form of control in our economy is competition. If a firm is faced with several strong competitors, it is unable to raise prices without losing customers to its competitors. However, the public utility companies do not have any competitors. Thus, it is necessary for the government to take the place of competition as a check against excessive prices.

It is important to note that government regulation of public utility rates is not equivalent to a price freeze. The rates are not frozen, they are regulated. Thus, the negative effects of price freezes which were discussed in the previous section do not apply to public utilities. If a public utility can effectively justify a rate increase to the regulatory agency, it will probably be permitted to increase its rates.

A strong argument could be made for extending this type of regulation to certain other key industries where price competition is minimal. While we do not have any cases of pure monopoly (a single seller) on a national basis, there are several key industries in which the degree of price competition is small indeed. For example, it has long been argued that there is little effective price competition in this country's steel industry. Allegedly, the various firms simply match or approximate the price increases announced by one of the largest firms, which they recognize as the price leader. If such is the case, one could argue for price controls on steel on the same basis that the public utilities are regulated.

A price increase in basic steel will probably result in a rise in prices for almost every single item containing steel. Thus, it is extremely important to avoid excessive price increases in basic industries where such increases will cause a whole chain of secondary price increases. There are only two ways to avoid such excessive price increases. Either strong competition or government controls are necessary. If it is true that many of our key industries lack sufficient competition to regulate prices effectively, then a strong case can be made for government action of some kind. One possibility would be government antitrust actions to break up some of the larger companies into smaller ones, thus increasing competition. The other option would involve some type of government controls similar to those used for public utilities.

While it is impossible and undesirable to control the prices of all firms in the nation, it is probably feasible to regulate prices effectively in those key industries where competition is insufficient to do the job. Guidelines could be established, such as the percentage of total industry sales by the top three or four companies, to determine which industries should receive regulation. Such regulation should not involve undue interference in the internal operations of the firms involved. A government agency would simply act as a watchdog to prevent excessive price increases. Price increases which could be justified on the basis of increased costs or below-average profits would be approved.

Most economists prefer to have prices controlled by competition rather than by the government. However, in those areas where there is insufficient competition to regulate prices effectively, limited government controls such as those described above are a possibility. They have worked rather well in the public utility industry for years.

Voluntary Controls. Voluntary controls on wages and prices have never proven very effective in this country. Generally speaking, voluntary controls are probably synonymous with no controls under most circumstances. It is unrealistic to expect individuals or businesses to agree voluntarily to a reduction in incomes, or even to maintaining their current incomes when they have the opportunity to increase them. An appeal from a strong and popular President during a time of crisis might cause some temporary restraint. However, in most cases voluntary controls are of little value.

Semivoluntary Controls. One possible compromise between voluntary controls and mandatory controls would involve the setting up of a standby authority and mechanism for regulating wages and prices. Such a standby authority could be used as an axe over the heads of companies and unions. So long as companies and unions acted responsibly in setting wages and prices, there would be no regulation. However, if wage and price increases became excessive, the regulatory agency would step in. The biggest criticism of this approach is that the standby regulatory agency would have too much power, in that it would decide what constituted irresponsible wage and price increases.

Long-Term Measures

In addition to the anti-inflationary measures already discussed, there are certain long-term measures which can be taken to diminish some of the underlying causes of inflation.

Measures to Increase Supplies and Productivity. One of the basic causes of inflation is insufficient supplies of goods and services to meet demands at current prices. For example, the tremendous increases in food and fuel prices in 1973 and 1974 were largely caused by shortages of these commodities. The obvious answer to this problem is to increase supplies, and reduce production costs by increasing productivity, in those areas where shortages exist. What can the government do along these lines? It can encourage increased production and productivity by supporting extensive research in these areas. Most of the big gains in productivity in the past have come from research, both private and public. In recent years the government has probably not been involved deeply enough in the promotion of research and development.

One of the most crucial fields in terms of research needs is the energy field. Scientists have been warning for years that an energy crisis would come unless extensive measures were taken to research and develop new sources of energy. Yet, only token efforts were made along these lines. Scientists warn today that the energy crisis of 1973-74 will be dwarfed by future crises unless we take extensive action now. They urge large federal expenditures for the funding of research on solar energy, nuclear energy, and various other potential energy sources for the future. Such research might prevent critical shortages of energy in the future and also the inevitable price increases that accompany such shortages.

Antitrust Actions. To the extent that inflation results from administered price increases in those industries with little effective price competition, a potential remedy would be to increase competition by breaking up some of the larger firms into smaller, more competitive firms. Many antitrust experts advocate such action.

It is often argued that you do not need a large number of firms to have effective competition. Some opponents of antitrust action will argue that three or four giant firms can provide just as effective competition as twenty small firms. While this could possibly be true in theory, it is not likely to work out in practice. The smaller the number of firms, the easier it is to get together and illegally agree on prices. Even if firms do not actually get together and fix prices, it is far more likely that three competitors will cooperate when you raise prices and match your price increases than would be the case with twenty competitors.

Antitrust action could easily be carried too far. In an advanced economy such as ours, large-scale production can lead to more efficient production at lower costs than would be the case on a small scale. For example, if our automobile industry consisted of one hundred firms of equal size rather than the present small number of large firms, automobiles would probably be more expensive and of poorer quality. If we had one hundred firms, there would be much greater competition, and profits might be much smaller. However, no firm could be large enough to take advantage of some of the economies of large-scale production which the present firms experience, and thus production costs and prices would probably be higher. However, the fact that one hundred automobile firms would be too many does not mean that three major firms are enough. Certainly we could have more than three major producers of automobiles without giving up the efficiencies of large-scale production.

In summary, many of our basic industries have only a few major firms. Antitrust action to split up some of the larger firms into smaller firms would probably increase the degree of competition and make excessive adminis-tered price hikes more difficult. However, it would be a mistake to create so many small firms that the economies of large-scale production would be lost.

Other Methods of Controlling Unemployment

We have already discussed in some detail the traditional weapons of monetary and fiscal policy for fighting unemployment. We have also discovered that they are not always totally successful in accomplishing full employment with stable prices. In this section we shall examine some other potential methods of reducing unemployment.

Other Fiscal-Policy Possibilities

In addition to the traditional fiscal-policy tools already discussed, there is a potential for the creation of some additional fiscal-policy instruments. One possibility for increasing investment spending during times of recession would be the creation of a tax-credit investment fund for corporations. A certain percentage of corporate income taxes could be set aside in a special fund. This portion of the tax would be refunded to those corporations who chose to use the funds for expansion purposes at certain critical times established by the government. In other words, during periods of insufficient aggregate demand the government would announce the release of these funds. A corporation could receive its tax-credit money only if it used the funds for expansion during the critical period stipulated by the government. Since monetary policy is usually ineffective in stimulating investment spending during times of recession, such a tax-credit fund might prove to be a very useful addition to the arsenal of anti-recession weapons.

Another possible innovation which could greatly increase the flexibility of fiscal policy would be the creation of a nonpartisan board of economic experts, similar to the Federal Reserve Board, which would be given authority to increase or decrease tax rates, within stipulated limits, for purposes of regulating aggregate demand. We have seen that the biggest problem of using tax increases and decreases as a regulatory device is the long delays that occur between the time a tax change is needed and the time such a change is enacted by Congress. We have also seen that political considerations are probably the major cause of such delays.

While increased interest rates are doubtless as unpopular as increased tax rates, the Federal Reserve Board can rapidly bring about a needed rise in interest rates without worrying about the political repercussions of such action. Since the Board members are appointed for fourteen-year terms and are ineligible for reappointment, their actions can be based solely on economic considerations as opposed to political considerations. Perhaps a similar board could be given the power to raise and lower tax rates within narrow limits. Congress could stipulate the exact limits within which tax rates were to be changed and would thus not be giving up its power of taxation by such action. This ability to increase or decrease taxes rapidly when needed, even within narrow limits, would greatly facilitate the regulation of aggregate demand, and thus the avoidance of excessive inflation or unemployment.

Government as the Employer of Last Resort

It is frequently asserted that every American has a basic right to have a good job and a decent income. However, during times of serious recession or depression millions of Americans are denied this "right." During such times, there are many advocates of the position that the government should serve as the employer of last resort. In other words, the government should make every effort to stimulate private employment, but if this fails to provide sufficient jobs, the government should employ those who remain unemployed.

Public works projects have long been controversial. Opponents argue that such projects often involve "make-work" activities which provide no lasting contribution to the economy and are thus wasteful. This argument need not be valid if government employment projects are set up and administered properly. There is nothing more wasteful than allowing an able-bodied man or woman who wants work to remain unemployed for a prolonged period of time. The basic needs of such individuals must be provided through public aid or private charity, and the individuals are not permitted to make any productive contribution to the economy. It is difficult to imagine any government employment project which could be more wasteful.

The source of these fears that government employment projects would be wasteful apparently goes back to the public employment projects during the depression of the 1930s. One often hears charges that some men were employed to dig holes and ditches and other men were hired to fill them back in. If such practices did indeed exist during the 1930s, they are to be deplored. The massive public works projects of the 1930s were organized hastily on a large scale, and some local administrators of these projects may have been lacking in good judgment and ethics. However, many of the projects of the 1930s were of such great value that we are still reaping the benefits some forty years later. Many beautiful public buildings still in use today were constructed with unemployed labor during the depression years. Country roads, city streets, parks, and playgrounds were constructed or improved. Flood control and irrigation dams were built. Scarcely a community can be found in this nation that did not receive some lasting benefits from the public works projects of the depression years.

Hence, there are many possibilities for beneficial public works projects. It is to be hoped that this nation will never again need anything approaching the massive public works projects of the depression years. However, government employment projects on a much smaller scale could be very useful at times such as the present, when efforts to fight inflation result in substantial unemployment.

Since beneficial public works projects take time to plan and implement, it is often suggested that the government should have standby projects that have been thoroughly planned and are ready to implement at any time. When the economy slips into recession and unemployment rises, these plans could be put into effect. Certainly, there are many such potential projects. We never have enough good highways, parks, and other recreation facilities. Also, there will probably always be a need for urban renewal. Why waste human resources during times of recession? Why not put the unemployed workers to work, providing valuable contributions to the economy and nation, and at the same time maintaining their incomes and self-esteem?

Labor-Market and Manpower Policies

Since the early 1960s, there has been an increased emphasis on policies designed to improve the functioning of labor markets, and to facilitate the proper development of manpower resources, as a means of reducing unemployment. Let us examine some potential labor-market and manpower policies which could lead to a reduction in unemployment.

The Need for a Better Job Clearance System.   We have already learned that full employment does not mean zero unemployment. Because there will always be some individuals who have just quit their job, just been fired, or just graduated from school, we must always have some unemployment. These individuals who are between jobs constitute frictional unemployment. How much frictional unemployment must the economy have? There is disagreement on this question. Some experts argue that we are capable of reducing unemployment to 3 percent of the labor force. Others believe that 4 percent should be considered "full employment," and a few even suggest that we should be satisfied with a 5 percent unemployment rate. The difference between a 3 percent unemployment rate and a 5 percent unemployment rate is substantial in terms of human suffering and lost production to the economy. With a civilian labor force of approximately ninety million individuals, a decline in unemployment from 5 percent to 3 percent would mean that 1.8 million more Americans would have jobs. This would also mean a substantial increase in the total production of goods and services by the economy.

Frictional unemployment can be reduced by reducing the time it takes to move from one job to another. Often an individual who has been fired, or has quit his job, will be unable to find a new job for several weeks or even longer. This may be due to a critical shortage of jobs in the area. However, it may also be due, at least partly, to the fact that the unemployed worker does not know how to go about finding a new job.

How does an unemployed person go about finding a new job? He may consult the classified ads in his local newspaper in search of job openings. However, statistics indicate that very few workers find jobs in this way. He may consult the State Employment Office, but again only a small percentage of workers find jobs through this means, since most employers do not list their vacancies with this agency. This leaves the unemployed worker with the necessity of simply going from firm to firm in search of a job opening.

Such a haphazard method of job hunting is inconsistent with our modern computer age. Yet, this is the only method available to most unskilled job seekers. What is needed is a central clearinghouse where all job vacancies in a given geographic area are listed. An unemployed worker could then get a list of all job vacancies in the area for which he was qualified and thus greatly reduce the time required to find a new job.

Most highly educated professional workers can find such services through both public and private placement agencies. However, the unskilled worker does not have a central job clearinghouse available to him. One frequent suggestion is that all employers be required to list their job vacancies, along with the job requirements, with their State Employment Office. An unemployed worker could then provide the State Employment Office with a list of his qualifications, and the computer could select a list of openings for which the worker was qualified. The worker could then apply for those jobs in which he was interested.

Employers have generally not listed many vacancies with the State Employment Office. They have instead preferred to fill vacancies with applicants who apply directly to the employer. They follow this practice for a variety of reasons, and there has been great reluctance on the part of the government to require them to list their vacancies. However, a listing of the vacancies would not necessarily require them to employ the applicants from the State Office. It would undoubtedly increase the number of applicants, and thus require more screening. However, this might also result in more highly qualified applicants. When we consider the potential gain to the economy from reduced frictional unemployment, the increased screening problem which employers would probably experience as a result of listing their vacancies with the State Employment Office does not seem very significant.

The Need for Better Career Guidance. We learned in Chapter 3 that structural unemployment involves either a skill mismatch or a geographic mismatch. In this and the next section we shall discuss ways of reducing structural unemployment which is caused by a skill mismatch. In the last section of this chapter we will consider solutions to the geographic mismatch problem.

A potential solution to the skill-mismatch problem involves better supply and demand projections for the various occupations, and an improved career guidance program which would communicate this information to young people before they begin their career training. While it is probably impossible to accurately predict the number of people who will enter a particular career field over the next ten years, it is possible to project the probable demand in the various fields with some degree of accuracy. The Bureau of Labor Statistics of the U.S. Department of Labor projects employment trends in nearly seven hundred specific occupations, for roughly a decade ahead, and publishes them in its *Occupational*

Outlook Handbook. In addition to projecting employment trends, this publication also describes the type of work involved and the training required for each of these occupations. Although it is not infallible, the *Occupational Outlook Handbook* should prove very helpful to young people who wish to make a rational career decision.

Unfortunately many young people choose a career without any objective information about employment prospects in the field. There is a serious lack of good career guidance both at the high school and college levels. Many students go through four years of high school and another four years of college without being exposed to the *Occupational Outlook Handbook.* Consequently, young people often enter into a long training period for an occupation which is already overcrowded. Thus, there is a critical need for improved career guidance. Young people should be adequately informed of the employment prospects in the various occupations while they are still in high school. Such action would certainly help to reduce structural unemployment of the skill-mismatch type.

Training and Retraining Programs. While a better career guidance program will help reduce the skill-mismatch problem among young workers, there will always be the problem of older workers whose skills have been replaced by technology. Many older unemployed workers are either unskilled or have obsolete skills. Therefore, there is a need for training and retraining programs for these workers. A number of federal programs have been developed in recent years which provide training and retraining opportunities for both young and older workers. Some of these programs provide for direct classroom instruction while others involve on-the-job training. There has been substantial criticism of some of these programs. However, they are making some contribution toward solving the structural unemployment problem.

Relocation Programs.   There are only two solutions to the problem of having unfilled job vacancies in one geographic area with qualified unemployed workers in another area. We must either move the jobs to the workers or move the workers to the jobs. Neither of these potential solutions is easy. However, some limited attempts have been made in recent years to relocate workers and/or jobs. The government has funded small pilot projects in which relocation allowances were paid to unemployed workers who were willing to move from labor surplus areas to labor shortage areas. These projects were generally regarded as successful, although it is important to note that many of the older unemployed workers are unwilling to move to a new location even with government moving allowances.

Attempts to encourage employers to move production units into labor surplus areas usually involve financial or other related incentives. Some programs have emphasized the construction of highways, airports, and other public facilities to make the area more accessible, and thus more attractive to businessmen. Other programs have emphasized special tax treatment or other financial incentives.

Summary

1. In addition to monetary and fiscal-policy measures, other methods of controlling inflation include various types of wage and price controls, antitrust actions to increase competition, and measures to increase production and productivity.

2. A permanent freeze on all wages and prices would be disastrous for the economy. Such a freeze would literally destroy the economic system and lead to unprecedented shortages. Fluctuating prices are the primary means of avoiding substantial shortages and surpluses in a free-market economy.

3. While it would be impossible and undesirable to control the prices of all firms in the nation, it would probably be feasible to effectively regulate prices in a few key industries where competition is insufficient to do the job. Public utility rates have been regulated by the government for years.

4. In addition to monetary and fiscal-policy measures, other methods of controlling unemployment include government employment projects, and improved labor-market and manpower policies.

5. Frictional unemployment can be reduced by reducing the time it takes to move from one job to another. A central clearinghouse where all job vacancies in a given geographic area were listed would speed up the process of finding a new job.

6. Improved supply and demand projections for the various occupations, combined with an improved career guidance program, could help reduce structural unemployment of the skill-mismatch type. Training and retraining programs for older workers can also help to reduce this type of unemployment.

7. Structural unemployment of the geographic-mismatch type can only be solved by either moving the jobs to the workers, or by moving the workers to the jobs. Some limited attempts have been made in recent years to relocate workers and jobs.

8 The Special Problems of the Seventies

The United States is faced with a combination of economic problems unique in American history. Early in 1975 the nation experienced some of the highest inflation in modern history, the highest unemployment since before World War II, and shortages of crucial items such as fuel and food. We have had periods of high inflation, periods of high unemployment, and periods of shortages. But never has the nation faced all three at the same time. We learned earlier in this book that actions taken to ease the unemployment problem usually contribute to increased inflation, and actions taken to fight inflation usually cause increased unemployment. While this trade-off relationship has always posed a serious dilemma for policy makers, never before has the dilemma been so great.

Historically the nation has usually suffered from either unemployment or inflation, but not both at the same time. When the economy is operating at full employment and suffering from inflationary pressures, it may be well worth the sacrifice of a small amount of unemployment in order to curtail the inflation. Similarly, when the problem is one of substantial unemployment with stable prices, a slight increase in prices is a small price to pay for reducing the jobless rate. However, today the rate of inflation and the level of unemployment are both already beyond what most experts consider the acceptable limits.

The Road Leading to the Special
Problems of the Seventies

How did the economy get into such a mess? Was it inevitable or could steps have been taken which would have enabled us to avoid this unfortunate predicament? These are questions on the minds of many Americans today. The answer to the second question is, no, the present economic situation was not inevitable. It could have been at least partially avoided if the proper actions had been taken at the right time. Certain aspects of the problem, such as adverse weather conditions and the oil embargo, may have been beyond the powers of the policy makers. However, much of the problem is due to sins of both omission and commission by two previous administrations. Let us examine some of the factors responsible for the current condition of the economy.

Failure to Curb Excess Demand During
the Late Sixties

The critical problem of inflation facing the nation in recent years had its beginning in 1966. Table 5 reveals that the period 1959 through 1965 was one of very little inflation. For seven years the annual rise in consumer prices was less than 2 percent. In 1965 prices rose by only 1.7 percent and unemployment was only 4.5 percent.

However, a chain of events beginning in 1966 was to lead the economy down a long road of inflation, and ultimately one of inflation and unemployment together. The escalation of the Vietnam War in 1966 led to a substantial unplanned upswing in military expenditures. This large increase in government spending caused aggregate demand to rise above the full-employment capacity of the economy, and the economy began a period of demand-pull inflation. Despite the advice of economists to raise taxes, the President and Congress procrastinated. It was not until 1968 that we got the 10 percent surtax. This tax increase probably helped, but it was more than two years too late to nip the inflationary

Table 5

The Road to Inflation and Unemployment

Year	Percent Increase[1] in Annual Average Consumer Prices	Percent Unemployment	
1959	.8	5.5	
1960	1.6	5.5	
1961	1.0	6.7	(Seven-year period of
1962	1.1	5.5	relatively stable
1963	1.2	5.7	prices.)
1964	1.3	5.2	
1965	1.7	4.5	
1966	2.9	3.8	(Period of upswing in
1967	2.9	3.8	Vietnam War spending and
1968	4.2	3.6	deficits totaling $37.7
1969	5.4	3.5	billion during time of full employment.)
1970	5.9	4.9	
1971	4.3	5.9	(Restrictive policies lead
1972	3.3	5.6	to increased unemployment
1973	6.2	4.9	but inflation continues.)
1974	11.0[2]	5.6	

[1]Consumer price increases reflect the change in the annual average consumer price index from one year to the next.

[2]During the twelve-month period December 1973 to December 1974, the consumer price index rose by 12.2 percent.

Source: U.S. Department of Labor, *Monthly Labor Review,* and Council of Economic Advisors, *Economic Report of the President.*

pressures in the bud. By 1968, prices had been rising so long that an inflationary psychology had developed in the nation.

It is easy to blame the Vietnam War for the inflation. However, it was not the war but the financing of the war that caused the inflationary problems. When military spending was accelerated in 1966, the economy was operating at the lowest level of unemployment in thirteen years. Not since 1953 had the unemployment rate dropped below 4 percent. Hence, the economy was operating near its maximum capacity output, and any increase in any component of aggregate demand would have to be offset by an equal decrease elsewhere or demand-pull inflation would occur. If the government demanded an increase in the production of military goods, there would have to be a corresponding decrease in the production of domestic goods. And any decrease in the production of consumer goods would have to be matched by an equal decrease in consumer spending if rising prices were to be averted.

Thus, economists argued for a tax increase to finance the increased military spending. Not only would the tax increase help to avoid deficits in the federal budget at a time of full employment, but it would also reduce the disposable income of consumers, and probably their level of spending. However, the President was reluctant to call for a tax increase to finance an increasingly unpopular war. When the President was finally convinced that a tax increase was absolutely necessary, Congress began to drag its feet. Thus, there was a delay of more than two years in getting a much-needed tax increase. By the time it finally came, inflation was too far out of control to be stopped by the small tax increase.

In our earlier discussion of fiscal policy we learned that federal deficits are in order during times of high unemployment and insufficient aggregate demand.

However, during times of full employment and inflationary pressures the budget should have a surplus. These fiscal policy guidelines were certainly violated during 1966, 1967, and 1968. During this three-year period, the federal government ran deficits totaling $37.7 billion. If these deficits had come during periods of high unemployment, they might have had a positive impact on the economy. However, at a time of full employment, they had a disastrous effect on the economy, and played a major role in building up the inflationary pressures which still plague us today. The economy was operating at full capacity, and thus was not capable of any significant increase in the production of goods and services. Yet the government pumped $37.7 billion more into the economy than it took out in the form of taxes during this three-year period. This huge increase in purchasing power, which could not be matched by a similar increase in the supply of goods and services, could only lead to rising prices.

In summary, our current problem of inflation began when the government failed to offset the large increase in Vietnam military spending with an appropriate tax increase in 1966. The excess aggregate demand resulting from this failure set the economy on a course of demand-pull inflation. By the time we got the surtax in 1968, an inflationary psychology had developed in the nation, and we were well on our way down the road to record peacetime inflation.

The Inflationary Psychology and
Administered Prices

After inflation has been allowed to develop unchecked for a prolonged period of time, a kind of inflationary psychology begins to develop in the nation. Consumers and businessmen tend to expect continued inflation and may increase their spending in an effort to beat future price increases. This, of course, adds fuel to the flames of inflation. Such an atmosphere also leads to increased administered-price inflation. During periods of stable prices, an exorbitant price increase in an industry with limited competition is more likely to be recognized for what it is. It may bring adverse reaction on the part of both government and consumers. However, during a period of generally rising prices throughout the economy, a firm can more effectively argue that an administered-price increase is necessary because of increased production costs. When most other prices are rising, it is difficult for firms with substantial market power to resist raising their prices, too, even in cases where profits are already abnormally high. Such firms may anticipate future cost increases, or possible future government price controls, and decide to raise prices while they still have the opportunity. Hence, inflation that begins primarily because of excess demand may soon become a mixture of demand-pull and administered-price inflation.

Such is the case with the current inflation. Tough monetary and fiscal policy measures might have been successful in bringing inflation under control in 1966 when it consisted primarily of demand-pull inflation. However, by the time the surtax came in 1968, an inflationary psychology had developed, and there was considerable administered-price inflation along with the demand-pull inflation. A strong fight should have been launched against administered-price inflation at that time. However, the government continued to rely primarily on monetary and fiscal-policy measures in the inflation fight up until August of 1971, when President Nixon announced the wage-price freeze.

Thus, the inflation which began in 1966 primarily as demand-pull inflation evolved into a mixture of excess-demand and administered-price inflation. The longer the inflation was allowed to persist, the more important administered-price inflation became as a part of the total problem. Hence, monetary and fiscal-policy measures are now insufficient to bring the inflation under control quickly without creating disastrously high unemployment. The restrictive monetary and fiscal-policy measures in the early Nixon years appear to have done more to increase unemployment than to reduce inflation. The attempt to slow the economy down gradually resulted in a rise in unemployment from 3.5 percent in 1969 to 5.9 percent in 1971. Yet inflation continued to be a problem. While monetary and fiscal policies can be very effective in controlling demand-pull inflation, their effectiveness on administered-price inflation is very limited. Consequently, the Nixon administration's efforts to curtail aggregate demand resulted in a rise in unemployment without the expected corresponding decrease in inflation. Hence, we ended up with the worst of both possible worlds, high inflation and high unemployment.

Shortages of Critical Items

The current economic mess is not completely due to the poor economic policies of the two previous administrations. In addition to the problems already discussed, the U.S. economy faced critical shortages of food and fuel, among other things, during 1973. Farm and food prices rose tremendously during 1973. This rise was caused primarily by a reaction to the reduced world output resulting from adverse weather in several parts of the world, including the United States. The poor weather conditions in other countries contributed to a tightening of world food markets, and the United States was faced with a huge increase in foreign demand as well as an increase in domestic demand. This excess demand for farm products caused food prices to rise by 20.1 percent during the twelve-month period from December 1972 to December 1973, as compared to an average rise of 8.8 percent for all items in the consumer price index.

Table 6
Regulations of the Controls Program, Phases II, III, and IV

Program	Phase II Nov. 14, 1971 to Jan. 11, 1973	Phase III Jan. 11, 1973 to June 13, 1973	Phase IV[1] Aug. 12, 1973 to Apr. 30, 1974
General Standards			
Price increase limitations—	Percentage pass-through of allowable cost increases since last price increase or Jan. 1, 1971, adjusted for productivity and volume offsets. Term limit pricing option available.	Self-administered standards of Phase II.	In most manufacturing and service industries dollar for dollar pass-through of allowable cost increase since last fiscal quarter ending prior to Jan. 11, 1973.
Profit limitations—	Not to exceed margins of the best two of three fiscal years before Aug. 15, 1971. Not applicable if prices were not increased above base level, or if firms "purified" themselves.	Not to exceed margins of the best two fiscal years completed after Aug. 15, 1968. No limitations if average price increase does not exceed 1.5 percent.	Same years as Phase III, except that a firm that has not charged a price for any item above its base price or adjusted freeze price, whichever is higher, is not subject to the limitation.
Wage increase limitations—	General standard of 5.5 percent. Exceptions made to correct gross inequities, and for workers whose pay had increased less than 7 percent a year for the last three years. Workers earning less than $2.75 per hour were exempt. Increases in qualified fringe benefits permitted raising standard to 6.2 percent.	General Phase II standard, self-administered. Some special limitations. More flexibility with respect to specific cases. Workers earning less than $3.50 per hour were exempted after May 1.	Self-administered standards of Phase III. Executive compensation limited.

Prenotification:			
Prices—	Prenotification required for all firms with sales above $100 million, thirty days before implementation, approval required.	After May 2, 1973, prenotification required for all firms with sales above $250 million whose price increase has exceeded a weighted average of 1.5 percent.	Same as Phase II except that prenotified price increases may be implemented in thirty days unless CLC requires otherwise.
Wages—	For all increases of wages for units of 5,000 or more; for all increases above the standard regardless of the number of workers involved.	None.	None.
Reporting:			
Prices—	Quarterly for firms with sales over $50 million.	Quarterly for firms with sales over $250 million.	Quarterly for firms with sales over $50 million.
Wages—	Pay adjustments below standard for units greater than 1,000 persons.	Pay adjustments for units greater than 5,000 persons.	As Phase III.
Special areas:	Health, insurance, rent, construction, public utilities.	Health, food, public utilities, construction, petroleum.	Health, food, petroleum, construction, insurance, executive and variable compensation.
Exemptions to price standards—	Raw agricultural commodities, import prices, export prices, firms with 60 or fewer employees.	Same as Phase II plus rents.	Same as Phase III plus manufactured feeds, cement, public utilities, lumber, copper scrap, long-term coal contracts, automobiles, fertilizers, nonferrous metals except aluminum and copper, mobile homes and semiconductors.

There was a second freeze on prices from June 13 to August 12.
Source: Cost of Living Council (CLC), from *1974 Economic Report of the President.*

The energy crisis, resulting at least partly from the Arab oil embargo, caused sharp increases in petroleum prices during 1973 and 1974. During the twelve-month period March 1973 to March 1974, gasoline prices rose by more than 40 percent, and fuel oil prices rose by more than 60 percent. Hence, shortages of both food and fuel have contributed substantially to the current problems of inflation.

Wage-Price Controls

On the evening of August 15, 1971, President Nixon, in a dramatic nationally televised address to the nation, announced a ninety-day freeze on wages, prices, and rents. This was the beginning of an attempt to control the U.S. economy artificially. It lasted for two years and eight months before controls were finally permitted to lapse in April 1974. The purpose of the surprise ninety-day freeze was to permit the development of a more durable program without giving prices and wages a chance to run away in anticipation of the new program. On November 14, 1971, the price freeze was replaced with Phase II of the wage-price control sequence. Phase II was replaced by Phase III on January 11, 1973. Phase III was followed by a second price freeze on June 13, 1973, and this was followed by Phase IV on August 12, 1973. Phase IV was the last stage of the control sequence which finally ended in April 1974. A general description of the regulations under Phases II, III, and IV is presented in Table 6.

How successful were the controls? It is obvious that the controls did not bring inflation under control. Whether or not inflation would have been even worse in the absence of the controls is open to argument. Some experts argue that the controls did have some restraining effect on inflation. However, others argue that the controls made the problem even worse. They contend that the controls caused distortions in the economy and resulted in many shortages which then further contributed to inflation.

Even President Nixon's own economic advisers had serious doubts that the control program had made much of a contribution in the fight against inflation. In its annual report submitted to the President in January 1974, the Council of Economic Advisers had this to say about the effectiveness of the controls:

> Controls could have worked in many ways, and economists' knowledge of the quantitative relationships determining prices is not so precise as to rule out the possibility that inflation might have been even greater in 1973 without controls. We think it would not have been much greater, however, since with the controls the rate of spending was high relative to the money supply, and output was low relative to the labor supply.
>
> Still no one can disprove the thesis that the controls had a significant effect, although 1973 makes it a hard thesis to believe. Doubts of this kind should come as no surprise. There is much prior evidence that price and wage controls of the kind tolerated during peacetime in free societies cannot significantly restrain inflation under the supply and demand conditions experienced in 1973.
>
> The effectiveness of controls obviously cannot be judged by 1973 alone. The operation of the controls during 1971 and 1972, bringing about a good balance in the structure of wages, may have helped to avoid a repetition in 1973 of the kind of wage spiral the country was experiencing before August 1971. On the other hand, if controls did hold down prices during 1973, the possibility remains that these prices will catch up in 1974 or later.[4]

The controls were probably destined to fail from the very beginning. Fluctuation prices serve a very useful purpose in a free market economy, and massive efforts to restrain prices artificially must inevitably result in distortions and shortages in the economy. However, this does not mean that absolutely no controls should ever be placed on the economy. The major problem with the Nixon control program was that it was far too compre-

---

[4]Council of Economic Advisers, *Economic Report of the President* (February, 1974), pp. 108-109.

comprehensive. It is both impossible and undesirable to control all prices in the economy artificially. In markets where there is sufficient competition to prevent administered price increases, there should be no controls. However, in basic industries where competition is limited and administered-price inflation is a problem, a case could be made for artificial controls at least during times of critical inflation.

In conclusion, the Nixon wage and price controls were unsuccessful in controlling inflation. They failed partly because they were too comprehensive, and also partly because they were poorly planned, poorly administered, and changed far too frequently. Counting the initial price freeze and a second freeze between Phases III and IV, there were five basic phases to the control program during the thirty-two months of control. Changes in the control program came so frequently that people found it difficult to keep informed about the current status of the controls. Certainly such instability in the control program did little to restore public confidence and price stability. A well-planned control program, limited to key industries where competition is limited and administered-price inflation is a problem, could be a useful supplement to monetary and fiscal policies in bringing inflation under control. Experience in the public utilities industry demonstrates that limited controls properly administered can work. However, the type of controls used by the Nixon administration probably do more harm than good.

Some Potential Courses of Action

When President Ford assumed office in August of 1974, he declared inflation our number one domestic enemy and seemed determined to wage a strong fight against it regardless of the consequences in terms of unemployment. He held an economic summit conference, proposed increased taxes, and asked Americans to curtail their spending, plant gardens, and wear WIN buttons. At that time unemployment was only 5.4 percent.

However, by early 1975 the unemployment picture had changed drastically. The unemployment rate for January 1975 was 8.2 percent, the highest rate since 1941, when World War II ended the Great Depression, and there was every indication that it was going even higher. The administration's own projections included an expected average unemployment rate of 8.1 percent for the entire year 1975, an expected 7.9 percent average rate for 1976, and rates above 6 percent until at least 1980. These predictions were astonishing when one considers the fact that the unemployment rate exceeded 6 percent in only two years during the entire post World War II period, with a 6.8 percent rate in 1958 and 6.7 in 1961.

Along with these dismal unemployment projections, the administration predicted that inflation would average 11.3 percent in 1975 and 7.8 percent in 1976. Furthermore, the administration expected a 3.3 percent drop in GNP for 1975.

Thus, by early 1975 the administration was recognizing the problem of recession and unemployment as at least equal in importance to the problem of inflation. President Ford's Economic Report to Congress in February 1975 begins as follows:

> The economy is in severe recession. Unemployment is too high and will rise higher. The rate of inflation is also too high although some progress has been made in lowering it.

The dual problems of high inflation and high unemployment do not lend themselves to easy solutions. However, the situation is not hopeless. Let us examine some possible courses of action.

Stimulate Aggregate Demand Through Monetary and Fiscal Policies

The most urgent problem facing the economy in early 1975 is the high unemployment rate. While the problems of inflation and energy are very serious long run problems, they do not pose the same degree of immediate danger that rapidly escalating unemployment does. Thus, immediate action is necessary to begin reversing the unemployment trend. With the proper policies, unemployment could be substantially reduced without contributing very much to inflationary pressures.

The decline in GNP and accompanying rapid rise in unemployment are due to insufficient aggregate demand. Whenever the total spending level is insufficient to purchase the total output currently being produced, the GNP will inevitably fall and unemployment will increase.

The obvious solution to a problem of insufficient aggregate demand is an increase in one or more of the components of aggregate demand. Consumption spending could be stimulated by reducing taxes, thus providing consumers with additional disposable income. Government spending could be increased, thus resulting in a direct increase in aggregate demand. Also, investment spending could theoretically be increased by lowering interest rates.

However, in actual practice it is difficult to encourage large-scale investment during times of severe recession even with lower interest rates. During recession most businessmen are faced with declining sales and are unwilling to expand capacity when they are unable to sell what they are currently producing. A more promising solution to sagging investment would involve tax credits and possible direct subsidation to the construction industry.

Since it is always difficult to stimulate investment during periods of recession, heavy reliance must be placed on increasing consumption and government spending. As consumer spending increases, businessmen will gradually begin to increase their investment as their sales approach the level of their maximum capacity to produce.

However, until that point is reached many businessmen will be unwilling to borrow for expansion purposes no matter how low the interest rate.

Any tax relief aimed at stimulating increased consumption must go to those consumers who will increase their spending and not their saving with the increased disposable income. Consumers in very high income brackets are likely to add part or all of any tax refund money to savings instead of increasing their spending. On the other hand, low income consumers will have a backlog of needs and probably will spend most or all of any tax relief money.

In addition to a tax cut for stimulating consumption, a strong case can be made for increased government spending. Increases in government spending have a direct and immediate effect on employment and can be directed toward those areas where the need is greatest. For example, a big increase in government funds going into housing could have a desirable effect on that hard-hit industry.

There is a common but fallacious belief that any increase in government spending will inevitably contribute to inflation. Increases in government spending are inflationary only when the economy is at or near full employment. For example, the accelerated spending on the Vietnam War in 1966-68 came at a time of the lowest unemployment in thirteen years. With unemployment running at 3.8 percent in both 1966 and 1967, the big increases in government spending at that time inevitably led to higher prices, since they were not offset by comparable reductions in consumption and/or investment spending.

However, the picture in early 1975 is different. With an unemployment rate of 8.2 percent, an increase in government spending should lead to increased production of goods and services and to increased employment without making any significant contribution to higher inflation. Government spending increases would be inflationary at a time of high unemployment only if the spending was in such a large amount that the economy moved too rapidly toward full employment or if it was channeled toward the purchase of scarce commodities such as fuel. If carefully implemented, government spending increases can be a powerful tool for lowering unemployment without substantially contributing to increased inflation.

Government Employment Projects

Unemployment causes hardships for both those individuals who are unemployed and for the economy as a whole. It also constitutes a waste of valuable productive resources and a loss in production to the economy. Hence, a strong case can be made for a government employment program which could put the unemployed workers to work on worthwhile projects which would make a lasting contribution to the nation.

We saw in Chapter 7 that, despite all the criticism that was aimed at the public works programs of the 1930's, many of the projects provided long-term benefits to the nation which we are still enjoying today. While public works projects do not provide a long-term solution to the unemployment problem, they do alleviate a great deal of human suffering in the short run while the longer term measures are taking effect. They also reduce the waste of unemployed resources that inevitably takes place during a recession.

Selective Wage-Price Controls

The current inflation is a mixture of excess-demand and administered-price inflation. The rising prices are partly due to shortages of certain items. When the demand for any item exceeds the available supply, the price will tend to rise. The only solution to this type of inflation is either to increase the supply or to decrease the demand. However, some of the current inflation is caused by businessmen who arbitrarily raise their prices even though there is no shortage of their product. This constitutes administered-price inflation, and it can best be controlled by limiting the discretion of the seller to set his own price, either through increased competition, or by means of artificial controls.

Antitrust action, as a means of increasing competition, is a possible long-run answer to administered-price inflation. However, selective controls offer a more immediate potential solution. At least until we get out of the current inflationary crisis, it might be desirable to reimpose selective wage-price controls on those large industries which produce key basic productive ingredients such as steel, aluminum, rubber, plastics, etc. Competition is limited in these areas and probably is not sufficient to prevent excessive administered price hikes.

A price increase for a basic ingredient such as steel or plastic will usually result in hundreds of other price increases for all those products which contain a substantial amount of that basic ingredient. For example, an increase in the price of basic steel will probably cause price increases in almost everything made from steel, including automobiles, appliances, construction materials, bicycles, wire, tools, and paper clips. It is impossible to control artificially the prices of all those items. However, it is not impossible to control the price of steel and other basic productive components. President Ford has asked for the restoration of the Cost of Living Council to monitor price increases. This will help to deter administered-price inflation. Perhaps we should go one step farther and reimpose controls on key industries where competition is weak.

Antitrust Actions to Increase Competition

A possible long-run solution to administered-price inflation is to increase competition by breaking up some of the giant corporations into smaller, more competitive firms through antitrust action. The greater the degree of competition, the more difficult it is for firms to engage in administered-price inflation. A businessman who faces many strong competitors in the sale of his product has little control over the price of his product. Strong antitrust action may not be politically easy. Most large firms have considerable influence in Washington and are often large contributors to political campaigns. Nevertheless, efforts should be made to increase competition wherever and whenever possible.

Selective Actions to Increase Output and Productivity

Excess-demand inflation can be eliminated either by decreasing the demand or by increasing the supply. Perhaps too much emphasis has been placed on reducing demand and too little on increasing supplies. Certainly there is a need to reduce the demand for such exhaustible items as oil and other fossil fuels. However, an equal effort should be made to increase the supplies of these and substitute items. Greater funding of research projects, designed to find new sources of scarce items and new and more efficient methods of production, could pay handsome returns in the future. Also, a strong case might be made for greater government subsidization in those fields where critical shortages exist.

American productivity (output per man hour) has not been growing nearly so rapidly in recent years as many experts believe it could. One of the causes seems to be low morale on the part of the workers. Many argue that our mass production methods make the worker feel that he is just a small unimportant cog in a large mechanism and deprive him of any pride in his job.

Various suggestions have been made for improving worker morale. Any successful efforts to increase worker productivity would lead to greater production at less cost and thus help to solve the inflation problem.

What Does the Future Hold for the U.S. Economy?

Despite the many problems facing the nation's economy today, the long-run outlook can be a bright one. Ours is a strong economy. No nation can match the combination of natural resources, plant and equipment, and highly educated manpower that the United States possesses. These are the things which make an economy strong. Our productive capacity is unequaled and unprecedented, and it is destined to continue to grow.

Nevertheless, a prolonged period of mismanagement of the economy could have disastrous long-run effects. It is extremely important that the current high unemployment and unprecedented peacetime inflation be brought under control. The economy will not cure itself. The present problems were brought on largely by mismanagement on the part of the government. It is now necessary for the government to take strong positive steps to restore the economy to health.

Government action must go far beyond attempts to solve the current economic problems. We need long-range planning and actions. Scientists are warning that the 1973-74 energy crisis was nothing compared to the energy crises of the future if we do not act now. We must begin now to take long-term actions to head off future energy crises. If we fail to do so, the future of our economy and our life styles are in great jeopardy.

The long-run planning must also put a heavy emphasis on the protection of our environment. Ignoring environmental safeguards in order to achieve short-term economic gains is like killing the goose that laid the golden egg. A healthy environment is essential to long-run economic health. Probably one of the most serious failings of our government in the past has been the failure to engage in long-term planning. We are a crisis nation. We wait until a crisis is upon us, and then we muster all the available resources to solve the problem that led to the crisis. We dare not wait until an environmental crisis is upon us. It may then be too late to solve the problem. We must begin now to make long-range plans for the future of our economy. We must anticipate crises before they come and take actions to offset them.

In conclusion, the future of our economy can be a bright one if a conscientious effort is made to solve the current problems, and anticipate and offset future problems. We have the basic resources necessary for a strong economy. Whether we will use them wisely, only the future can tell. There is no foolproof blueprint for proper management of the economy. However, one ingredient of any successful approach must include long-range considerations.

Summary

1. We are today facing some of the most difficult economic problems to face the nation since the depression of the 1930s. We are facing problems of inflation, unemployment, and critical shortages all at the same time.

2. The current economic mess is due to a variety of factors. Certain factors, such as adverse weather conditions and the oil embargo, were probably beyond the powers of the policy makers. However, much of the problem is due to sins of both omission and commission by two previous administrations.

3. The failure to curb excess demand during the late sixties bears a lot of responsibility for the current economic mess. The prolonged period of excess demand allowed strong inflationary pressures to build up.

4. The wage-price controls of the Nixon administration failed partly because they were too comprehensive, and also partly because they were poorly planned, poorly administered, and changed far too frequently.

5. Some potential courses of action for solving the current problems include: stimulating aggregate demand through monetary and fiscal policies; government employment projects; selective wage-price controls; antitrust actions to increase competition; and selective actions to increase output and productivity.

6. Despite the many problems facing the nation's economy today, the long-run outlook can be a bright one if the economy is properly managed. We have the resources to remain a very strong economy. However, a prolonged period of mismanagement of the economy could have disastrous long-run effects.

Appendix

Some Basic Tools of Economic Analysis

Throughout this book we have avoided technical analysis in favor of an elementary verbal approach. The purpose of this appendix is to provide those readers who are interested in a more technical comprehension of the subject with an introduction to some of the fundamental analytical tools. A mastery of these basic analytical concepts should be helpful to those readers who wish to read some of the more technical literature in the field.

Supply and Demand Analysis

Economists usually use the basic supply and demand model to illustrate the effects of changing supply and demand. It is a very useful analytical tool, and the reader who plans to read more advanced works in economics may find it a prerequisite to the understanding of such works.

The Supply and Demand Model

In Table A-1 a hypothetical demand schedule for corn is presented. The term "demand" refers to the whole schedule of quantities that will be bought at different possible prices. If we refer to a specific quantity that will be bought at a specific price, we use the phrase "quantity demanded." In other words, the quantity demanded at a price of $5 is 100 million bushels per month. The quantity demanded at a price of $4 per bushel is 150 million bushels per month. At a price of $3 per bushel, 200 million bushels per month will be purchased, and so forth. Again, the quantity demanded refers to a specific quantity that will be purchased at a specified price, and demand refers to the whole schedule of possible price and quantity combinations.

Table A-1
Demand Schedule for Corn
(hypothetical data)

Price ($ per bu.)	Quantity Demanded (Million bu. per mo.)
$5	100
4	150
3	200
2	250
1	300

The data from Table A-1 are plotted in the diagram in Figure A-1 to produce a demand curve.[5] Price is measured on the vertical axis, and quantity is measured on the horizontal axis of the demand model. You will note that the demand curve slopes downward to the right, indicating that larger quantities will be purchased at lower prices and smaller quantities at higher prices. For

---

[5]For simplicity the supply and demand curves in this appendix are drawn as straight lines although they usually have some curvature to them.

example, at the high price of $5 per bushel only 100 million bushels of corn per month will be purchased. However, at a low price of $1 per bushel, 300 million bushels will be purchased per month.

The specific amounts that will be purchased at the various possible prices in this hypothetical demand curve may or may not be realistic. However, there is no doubt that larger quantities of corn would be purchased at low prices than at high prices. The principle of the downward-sloping demand curve holds true for almost all items.

Figure A-1: Demand Curve for Corn

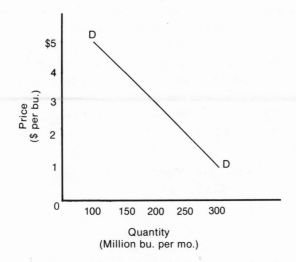

In Table A-2, a hypothetical supply schedule for corn is presented. Again, the term "supply" refers to the whole schedule of quantities that will be supplied at various possible prices, and the phrase "quantity supplied" refers to a specific quantity that will be supplied at a specific price.

Table A-2
Supply Schedule for Corn
(hypothetical data)

Price ($ per bu.)	Quantity Supplied (Million bu. per mo.)
$5	300
4	250
3	200
2	150
1	100

The data in Table A-2 are presented as a supply curve in Figure A-2. Again, price is measured on the vertical axis, and quantity is measured on the horizontal axis. The supply curve upslopes to the right, indicating that suppliers will be willing to supply larger amounts at higher prices and smaller amounts at lower prices. For example, at a price of $5 per bushel, 300 million bushels per month will be supplied, and at the low price of $1 per bushel suppliers would be willing to supply only 100 million bushels per month. Again, the specific quantity and price combinations listed in this hypothetical example may or may not be realistic. However, the fact that the quantity supplied will increase as the price increases is very realistic.

Figure A-2: Supply Curve for Corn

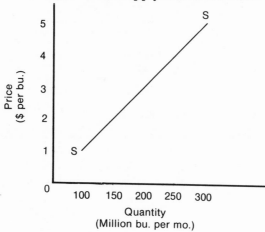

In Table A-3 the supply and demand schedules are put together to determine the equilibrium price. The equilibrium price is that price at which the quantity demanded is exactly equal to the quantity supplied. In our hypothetical example the equilibrium price of corn is $3 per bushel. At a price of $3 the quantity that will be bought is 200 million bushels per month, and the quantity that will be offered for sale is also 200 million bushels per month. There is neither a surplus nor a shortage at this price. At any price other than $3 per bushel there will be either a surplus or a shortage. For example, at a price of $4 per bushel suppliers will want to sell 250 million bushels per month while only 150 million bushels will be purchased. At a price of $2 per bushel purchasers will want to buy 250 million bushels per month while suppliers will be willing to sell only 150 million bushels. At prices which are too high for equilibrium, the existence of a surplus will tend to force prices down. At prices below the equilibrium level, the resulting shortage will tend to cause prices to rise as buyers compete with each other for the short supply. Therefore, market forces will tend to move the price toward the equilibrium level of $3 per bushel.

Table A-3
Supply and Demand Schedules for Corn
(hypothetical data)

Price ($ per bu.)	Quantity Demanded (Million bu. per mo.)	Quantity Supplied (Million bu. per mo.)	
$5	100	300	Price too high for equilibrium. (Q supplied exceeds
4	150	250	Q demanded.)
3	200	200	Equilibrium
2	250	150	Price too low for equilibrium (Q demanded exceeds
1	300	100	Q supplied.)

In Figure A-3 the data from Table A-3 are presented in the form of supply and demand curves. You will again note that the demand curve slopes downward to the right, indicating that increased quantities will be purchased as the price declines. The supply curve, on the other hand, slopes upward to the right, indicating that smaller and smaller quantities will be supplied as the price falls. The one unique point on the diagram where the two curves intersect is the *equilibrium point.* The *equilibrium price* is $3 per bushel and the *equilibrium quantity* is 200 million bushels per month. At prices above $3 per bushel a surplus exists. At prices below $3 per bushel there is a shortage. Only at the price of $3 per bushel is the quantity demanded exactly equal to the quantity supplied.

**Figure A-3: Supply and Demand
Curves for Corn, and Equilibrium
Price and Quantity Determination**

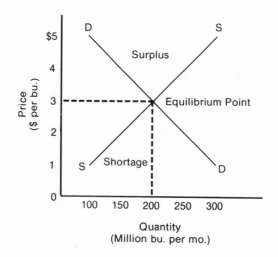

Changes in Supply and Demand

Now that the basic supply and demand model has

been developed, we can use it to explain many price changes. Supply and demand do not usually remain fixed . for any extended periods of time. Changes in tastes, changes in incomes, changes in the availability and prices of substitute items, etc., cause demand to fluctuate from time to time. Supply is also frequently changing due to changes in production methods and costs, changes in weather conditions, etc. Suppose that an unusually good growing season causes the harvest of this year's corn crop to be substantially higher than expected. Figure A-4 depicts such a situation. The supply curve shifts to the right, indicating that larger amounts will be offered for sale at all prices than before. The new supply curve S²S² intersects the unchanged demand curve at a price of $2 per bushel instead of $3. The increase in supply has reduced the equilibrium price.

Figure A-4
Price Effect of an Increase in Supply

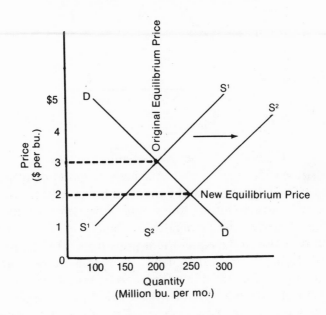

In Figure A-5 the reverse situation is presented. If, due to poor weather conditions, insect damage, or disease, the corn yield is substantially below normal, the supply curve will shift to the left. In this example, the equilibrium price would rise from $3 to $4 per bushel. Thus, if demand remains unchanged, an increase in supply will tend to force prices down, and a decrease will force prices up.

Figure A-5
Price Effect of a Decrease in Supply

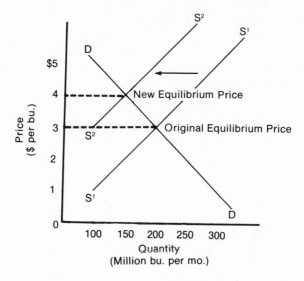

Quantity
(Million bu. per mo.)

In Figures A-6 and A-7, changes in demand are illustrated. If as a result of increased exports or other factors, total purchases of corn at all prices tend to rise, this will cause a shifting to the right of the demand curve as illustrated by the curve D^2D^2 in Figure A-6. The result will be a rise in the equilibrium price from $3 to $4 per bushel. If, on the other hand, there is a decrease in demand as illustrated by Figure A-7, the equilibrium price will fall from $3 to $2 per bushel. Thus, if supply is unchanged, an increase in demand will tend to increase

Figure A-6
Price Effect of an Increase in Demand

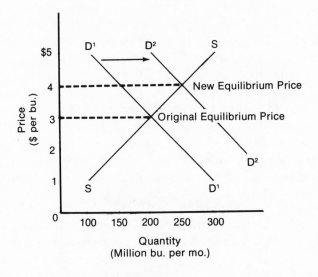

Figure A-7
Price Effect of a Decrease in Demand

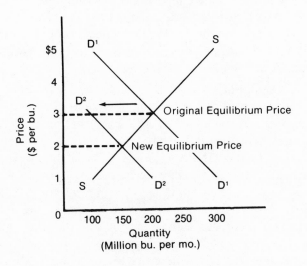

prices and a decrease in demand will have a depressing effect on prices.

In summary, prices tend to be forced up by increases in demand and / or decreases in supply, both of which will result in shortages if prices do not adjust upward. Prices tend to be forced down by decreases in demand and / or increases in supply, both of which usually lead to surpluses. Thus, many cases of price increases are easily explained by simple supply and demand factors. If there is a shortage of an item at current prices, then prices will tend to rise until the shortage is eliminated. If artificial price controls prevent the price from rising to its equilibrium level, the shortage will continue indefinitely.

The Aggregate Demand Model

We learned earlier in this book that aggregate demand consists of the total of consumption spending, plus investment spending, plus government spending. We also learned that aggregate demand (C + I + G) must equal total output (GNP) in order for GNP to remain stable. If aggregate demand is greater than GNP, there will be an increase in GNP either in real terms or in money terms. Conversely, if aggregate demand is less than GNP, there will be a decline in GNP. The relationship between aggregate demand and GNP is presented in Table A-4 and Figure A-8, using hypothetical data.

In examining the data in Table A-4 you will note that only at an output of $850 billion does aggregate demand equal GNP. At levels of GNP above $850 billion, the total output exceeds the total spending, and thus there will be a reduction in the GNP. At levels of GNP below $850 billion, the total spending exceeds the total output, and there will be an increase in GNP. At an output of $850 billion, the economy is in equilibrium. That is, the total spending just equals the total output, and thus there will be no tendency for GNP to change unless there is a change in aggregate demand. There are forces at work always

Table A-4
Aggregate Demand Schedule
(hypothetical data)

Gross National Product (GNP) (billions)	Consumption Spending (C) (billions)	Investment Spending (I) (billions)	Government Spending (G) (billions)	Aggregate Demand (C+I+G) (billions)	
$950	670	100	140	910	Total Output Exceeds Total Spending
900	640	100	140	880	
850	610	100	140	850	Equilibrium C+I+G = GNP
800	580	100	140	820	Total Spending Exceeds Total Output
750	550	100	140	790	

moving the economy toward this equilibrium position.

It is extremely important to understand that there is nothing necessarily good about equilibrium. If the economy is in equilibrium at the full-employment level of output, that is great. However, the economy can be in equilibrium at a time of substantial unemployment. Equilibrium simply means that the economy is producing an amount equal to the amount of goods and services that are being purchased. If aggregate demand is extremely low, the GNP will also be low, and unemployment will be high. If aggregate demand is high, GNP will be high, and unemployment will be low. In other words, the GNP adjusts to a level consistent with the level of total spending at any given point in time.

The hypothetical data from Table A-4 are presented in the form of the basic aggregate demand model in Figure A-8. This basic model can be very useful in understanding the effects of insufficient or excessive aggregate demand. Aggregate demand (C + I + G) is measured on the vertical axis, and the level of GNP is measured on the horizontal axis. The 45 degree line is a helping line which indicates points where C + I + G = GNP. You will note that, since the scales of the two axes are identical, any point on the 45 degree line is a point where the amount on the vertical axis is identical to the amount on the horizontal axis. Thus, the point where the aggregate demand line (C + I + G) crosses the 45 degree line is the point of equilibrium. At that point, and only at that point, C + I + G = GNP. In our example, that point is at a level of $850 billion.

Inflationary and Deflationary Gaps

In Figure A-9, three hypothetical aggregate demand schedules are presented. The desirable schedule is (C + I + G)[1] since it crosses the 45 degree line at the full-employment level of GNP. In other words, with (C + I + G)[1] the economy is in equilibrium at full employment. Unfortunately, the economy seldom operates at

Figure A-8
Aggregate Demand Model

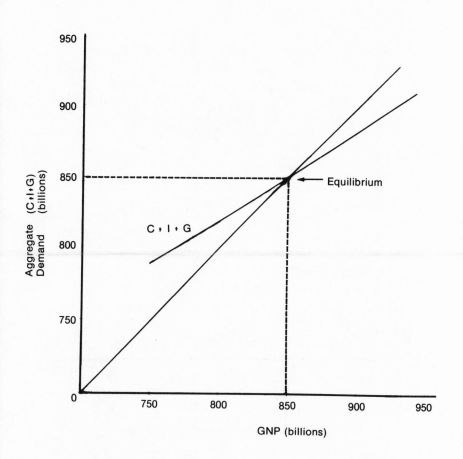

Figure A-9
Inflationary and Deflationary Gaps

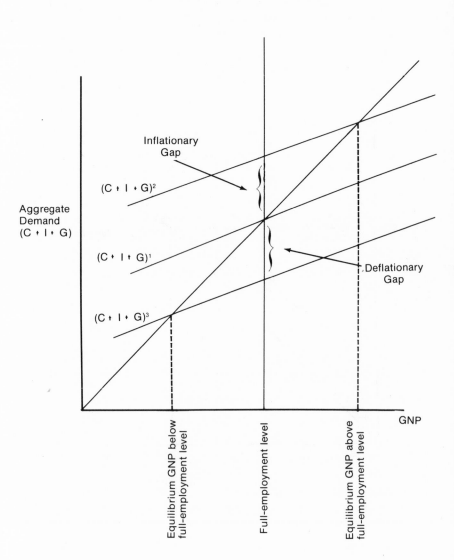

exactly this level. Usually, aggregate demand is either too high or too low to be in equilibrium at the full-employment level of GNP.

The $(C + I + G)^2$ aggregate demand schedule in Figure A-9 is too high for equilibrium at full employment, and an inflationary gap exists. The inflationary gap is measured at the full-employment level of GNP. It measures the amount by which actual aggregate demand exceeds the aggregate demand necessary for the economy to be in equilibrium at full employment.

With the $(C + I + G)^3$ schedule, aggregate demand is too low for equilibrium at full employment, and a deflationary gap exists. The deflationary gap measures the amount by which actual aggregate demand falls short of the aggregate demand necessary for the economy to be in equilibrium at full employment.

Policy makers attempt to close inflationary and deflationary gaps by using monetary and fiscal policies to change the level of aggregate demand. Unfortunately, this task is more difficult than it appears. It is possible to have a deflationary gap and still have substantial inflation of the administered-price type. Also, it is not possible to accurately determine the exact changes in monetary and fiscal policy necessary to bring the economy to full-employment equilibrium.

The Multiplier

We have seen that changes in consumption spending, investment spending, and government spending constitute changes in aggregate demand and thus in national income.[6] The multiplier principle states that changes in spending bring about magnified changes in national income. For example, an increase in investment spending of $1,000 will result in an increase in national income of more than $1,000. If the $1,000 of new

---

[6]Although there is a more technical definition, the expression "national income" is generally considered synonymous with GNP.

investment results in an increase in national income of $2,000, the multiplier is 2. If income increases by $2,500, the multiplier is 2.5, and if the income change is $3,000, the multiplier is 3. The multiplier is the number by which the change in spending must be multiplied to get the resulting change in income.

The size of the multiplier is determined by the marginal propensity to consume. The marginal propensity to consume (MPC) is a measure of the change in consumption spending that will take place as a result of a given change in income. It measures the additional consumption spending which results from an additional dollar of income. If consumers on the average will spend sixty cents and save forty cents out of each additional dollar of income, the marginal propensity to consume is .6 and the marginal propensity to save is .4. If consumers tend to spend seventy cents and save thirty cents out of each additional dollar of income, the marginal propensity to consume is .7 and the marginal propensity to save is .3. If consumers spend eighty cents and save twenty cents out of each additional dollar of income, the marginal propensity to consume is .8 and the marginal propensity to save is .2.

A simple example can reveal why a change in spending leads to a multiplied change in national income. Suppose you hire an unemployed worker to do $1,000 worth of repairs, and suppose the marginal propensity to consume is .8. The worker will respend $800 of the $1,000 you pay him. Those individuals who receive the $800 from the worker will tend to spend $640 (.8 x $800). In the next round of spending there will tend to be $512 (.8 x $640) spent. This spending chain will continue, ultimately generating as much as $5,000 in total income. In other words, the $1,000 you paid the unemployed worker resulted in an increase of $5,000 in national income with a multiplier of 5.

There is a simple formula for obtaining the multiplier. The multiplier $= \dfrac{1}{1\text{-MPC}} = \dfrac{1}{\text{MPS}}$. The multiplier is simply the upside-down or "reciprocal" of the marginal propensity to save (MPS). Hence, when the MPC is .8, the MPS must be .2 or $\dfrac{2}{10}$. The reciprocal (upside-down) of $\dfrac{2}{10}$ is $\dfrac{10}{2}$ which is 5. Thus, with a marginal propensity to consume of .8, the multiplier is 5. If the MPC were .9, the MPS would be $\dfrac{1}{10}$ and the multiplier would be $\dfrac{10}{1}$ or 10. If the MPC were .5, the MPS would be $\dfrac{5}{10}$ and the multiplier would be $\dfrac{10}{5}$ or 2.

The multiplier concept is very significant. It means that if during a recession the GNP is $50 billion below the full-employment level, total spending does not have to increase by $50 billion in order to remove the deflationary gap. If the multiplier is 5, only $10 billion of additional spending is necessary to bring the economy to full employment.

Index